The Edible Flower
Garden

The Edible Flower Garden

From garden to kitchen: *choosing, growing and cooking edible flowers*

KATHY BROWN Photographs by Michelle Garrett

HERMES HOUSE

This edition is published by Hermes House,
an imprint of Anness Publishing Ltd
info@anness.com
www.hermeshouse.com
www.annesspublishing.com

If you like the images in this book and would like to investigate using
them for publishing, promotions or advertising, please visit our website
www.practicalpictures.com for more information.

© Anness Publishing Limited 2022

A CIP catalogue record for this book is available from
the British Library.

Publisher: JOANNA LORENZ
Editorial Director: HELEN SUDELL
Senior Editor: LINDSAY PORTER
Designer: LISA TAI
Photographer and Stylist: MICHELLE GARRETT
Home Economist: JOANNA FARROW
Production Controller: BEN WORLEY

PUBLISHER'S NOTE
Although the advice and information in this book are believed to be accurate at the time of going to
press, neither the authors nor the publisher can accept any legal responsibility or liability for any
errors or omissions that may have been made nor for any inaccuracies nor for any loss, harm or
injury that comes about from following instructions or advice in this book. Do not eat herbs or
flowers if you have a medical condition, without appropriate advice. The book suggests you cultivate
rather than pick wild flowers. Do not pick flowers you are unsure about identification. Do not pick
wild flowers which are endangered, such as cowslips (their status can vary), and follow local by-laws.
Do not eat flowers picked from the roadside, or those that have been treated with pesticides. Please
note that certain individuals, particularly those with pollen allergies, may suffer adverse reactions to
eating flowers.

COOK'S NOTES
Bracketed terms are intended for American readers.
For all recipes, quantities are given in both metric and imperial measures and,
where appropriate, in standard cups and spoons. Follow one set of measures, but
not a mixture, because they are not interchangeable. Standard spoon and cup
measures are level.
1 tsp = 5ml, 1 tbsp = 15ml, 1 cup = 250ml/8fl oz.
Australian standard tablespoons are 20ml. Australian readers should use 3 tsp
in place of 1 tbsp for measuring small quantities.
American pints are 16fl oz/2 cups. American readers should use 20fl oz/
2.5 cups in place of 1 pint when measuring liquids.
Electric oven temperatures in this book are for conventional ovens. When using a
fan oven, the temperature will probably need to be reduced by about
10–20°C/20–40°F. Since ovens vary, you should check with your manufacturer's
instruction book for guidance.
Medium (US large) eggs are used unless otherwise stated.

Introduction

So often gardeners love to cook, especially crops they have grown themselves. It is also true that many cooks like to garden, especially the herbs that can flavour their food. In this unique book the arts of gardening and cooking become partners. The two skills are brought together for the benefit of all, with recipes for planting schemes and culinary treats discussed in tandem. The edible flower garden will become a new challenge for gardeners and cooks alike.

This is a book for both new and experienced gardeners and cooks. These recipes combine new ways of growing old favourites, both in containers and in the ground, with new ways of using them in the kitchen. The step-by-step approach means that everyone can both garden and cook.

Many of the flowers featured can be easily grown in just one summer. Nasturtiums, courgettes (zucchini), borage, sunflowers and pot marigolds will all provide masses of colour from just one sowing. They can be grown in the ground or in containers and are as versatile in the kitchen as they are in the garden. Just choose whether you want yellow or green courgettes, or whether you want dwarf or tall sunflowers. You might want semi-trailing nasturtiums in a window-box but tall ones climbing up a fence. In the past you might have despaired when your rocket (arugula) or basil came into flower, as it meant that there would be less succulent leaves. But now you will be pleased and learn to enjoy a whole new crop of wonderful tasty flowers.

No doubt because of its ease and versatility, the fashion for container gardening just gets stronger and stronger and edible flowers can be grown in containers in the most delightful ways. Try bergamot in a barrel with other tea plants such as peppermint and lemon balm or a combination of strawberry plants in a pot with flowering marjoram. A cowslip basket with an underplanting of violas is a beautiful herald of spring and the resulting blooms can be scattered

over salads or crystallized to decorate cakes. Another idea for spring would include cowslips, daisies, violas and rosemary as well as mints and marjoram to flower later in the season. A summer-herb basket might be filled with edible alpine pinks, flowering thymes, lavender and mints.

Flowers have been used for culinary purposes for centuries – flowers were pickled or candied, made into syrup, used on salads, or transformed into wine or cordials.

Modern ways of cooking are not nearly so elaborate or time-consuming as the methods employed in previous decades and centuries, and many of the edible ideas given here are instant in their results. The flowers are used as a beautiful garnish or addition and are fresh, fragrant and flavoursome at the same time. This is deliberate on the one hand, because modern lifestyles require a quick and easy approach, but is it also one of the best ways to use them. Visual attractiveness or "eye appeal" is surely one of the most important aspects of preparing food. A few borage flowers will give a whole new look to a summer fruit plate and a handful of nasturtium flowers scattered over a salad of garden leaves will completely transform it, not only in appearance, but in texture and flavour as well.

Some of the cookery recipes involve more time in the kitchen, but they are certainly worth it. The rose ice bowl and the rose sorbet, for example, are both made over a matter of hours, but I think you will agree, the results are spectacular. Floral oils and vinegars may sound complicated but actually take very little time at all. Crystallizing petals takes a little longer perhaps, but with a paintbrush in hand, the whole exercise can be very therapeutic and the results taste absolutely delicious.

As well as the specific gardening and culinary recipes, I am sure you will find a good use for the Plant Directory at the back of the book, which gives you all the information you need on how best to grow and use a particular edible flower in the kitchen.

I hope that, by looking at growing and cooking edible flowers in conjunction, this book succeeds in opening your eyes and imagination to a wealth of new scents, sights, textures and tastes.

Kathy Brown

Clockwise from far left: Marjoram flowers add flavour to pizza; a summer basket filled with herbs and alpine pinks; crystallized cowslips and violas for dessert; a pot of roses and anchusa.

rose-water **rose oil**

violet conserve

hyssop syrup

cowslip paste

preserved borage

orange-flower brandy

saffron cordial

syrup of flowers

Edible Flowers in History

In centuries past, flowers have been held in great esteem both for their scent and flavour. The Romans used mallows, fennel, alpine pinks, violets and roses in their dishes as well as lavender in their sauces, but they were by no means the first. Pot marigolds and orange blossom have been used for over a thousand years in Eastern cooking, while lilies and chrysanthemums have been used for even longer.

Right: *One of the oldest species of rose, Rosa Mundi, still flourishes today. Its strong scent makes it equally welcome in the kitchen and garden.*

Flowers in the Pantry

In the 16th century, Europe experienced an unprecedented interest in gardening and garden design – and the ladies of wealthy estates had become very knowledgeable about growing, using and conserving flowers in the home. With the exploration of new lands, many foreign plants were introduced to Europe, resulting in a great cross-fertilization of knowledge between the New and Old Worlds. These were exciting times, and fortunately much has been recorded.

The Tudor still-room had been a major force in the art of using herbs and edible flowers, and the practices continued and reached new heights of ornamentation in the Stuart era of the 17th century. But somewhere between the heyday of the 16th and 17th centuries and the middle of the 19th century, the skills were largely lost.

When Eleanour Sinclair Rohde (1881–1950) wrote *A Garden Of Herbs* in 1920 it was to instruct readers about growing and using herbs as had been done in the past. As an historian with a passionate interest in herb gardens, she designed a garden in 1919 and read many of the original texts of the 16th, 17th and 18th centuries. She not only knew what would have been grown to furnish the Tudor and Stuart still-rooms of the great houses but also learnt exactly how the fruit, vegetables and flowers would have been used. She had made a detailed study of the recipe books, or 'receipt books' as they were then called, of some of the famous royal cooks of those times. These included Joseph Cooper, cook to Charles I who wrote a receipt book dated 1654, and a cook recorded only as W.M., who was cook to Charles I's wife, Queen Henrietta Maria from France, and who wrote *The Queen's Closet Opened* in 1655. Eleanour Rohde also read William Rabisha's *The Whole Body of Cookery Dissected* (1675), John Evelyn's *Acetaria* (1699) and E. Smith's *The Compleat Housewife* (1736) among many other texts.

Below: *A 16th-century allegorical painting depicts spring as a lady of the manor surrounded by floral bounty.*

Through her detailed research we are able to glimpse into the kitchens and still-rooms of the 16th and 17th centuries – treasure troves of wonderful scents and flavours. There, a stove would always be kept burning to keep the atmosphere warm and dry, just right for drying and storing all the herbs and flowers needed for the household. These supplies went to make the herbal remedies on which everyone depended and which formed the basis of all the fragrant powders and soaps, polishes and washballs used throughout the house. Here, too, lay the beginnings of so many culinary delights.

In houses great and small, the pantry would have been quite different from any we know of today. There would be bottles of rose-water and rose oil. Glass jars would contain vinegars flavoured with roses, cowslips, gillyflowers (the old name for clove-scented alpine pinks and carnations) and violets. There would be floral conserves and syrups made from roses, violets, borage, lavender, rosemary and bugloss flowers as well as boxes of candied flowers such as pot marigolds cut into wedges "Spanish fashion", sugared pastes of cowslips and many other treats.

Above: A 19th-century still-life of pansies and pelargoniums, two species of edible flower still enjoyed today.

candied flowers

The art of preserving flowers in sugar was a great favourite. Sometimes the petals, or alternatively whole flowers, would be sugared individually. On other occasions they would be made into "drops" or "sugar paste" to be cut and eaten as we would eat candies today.

We are able to learn from W.M., cook to Queen Henrietta Maria, wife of Charles I of England, how "To Candy Borage, Or Rosemary Flowers":

Boil sugar and Rose-water a little upon a chafing-dish with coales; then put the flowers (being thorowly dried, either by the Sun or by the Fire) into the Sugar, and boile them a little: then strew the powder of double refined Sugar upon them, and turne them, and let them boile a little longer, taking the dish from the Fire: then strew more powdered Sugar on the contrary side of the flowers. These will dry of themselves in two or three houres in a hot sunny day, though they lie not in the Sunne.

William Rabisha recorded in *The Whole Body of Cookery Dissected* (1675) how "To Candy Rose Leaves As Natural As If They Grow On Trees." He advises to spread red or damask rose petals out on paper, and sprinkle with rose-water and fine sugar. They should be left out in the sunshine to allow the sun to candy the sugar. The process is repeated several times on both sides until they have dried and candied.

In the same book, he describes how "To Candy All Manner Of Flowers In Their Natural Colours":

Take the flowers with the stalks, and wash them over with a little Rose-water, wherein Gum-Arabick is dissolved; then take fine searsed sugar, and dust over them, and set them a drying on the bottom of a sieve in an oven, and they will glisten as if it were Sugar-Candy.

Although many recipes used just one flower, others included a rich assortment. Often they would be of the same season but sometimes the flowers of spring and summer were used together. This could only have been possible where all or some of the flowers had been preserved, which may account for the large number of recipes for candying flowers. The following recipe from the 1723 title, *The Receipt Book of John Nott*, Cook to the Duke of Bolton, uses mixed-season flowers:

Mince cowslip flowers, clove, gillyflowers, rose petals and Spinach of each a handful, take a slice of Manchet [white bread] and scald it with cream. Add a pound of blanch'd Almonds pounded small with Rose-water, a quarter of a Pound of Dates sliced and cut small, the yolk of three eggs, a handful of Currants and sweeten all with Sugar. When boiled pour Rose-water over and scrape Sugar on. Then serve up.

floral drinks

One of the other very common ways in which flowers were used was to flavour drinks such as cordials, wines, liqueurs and brandy. This 18th-century recipe for adding fragrant orange flowers to brandy sounds delicious: "To Make Orange-Flower Brandy", says E. Smith in *The Compleat Housewife* (1736), "Take a gallon of French Brandy, boil a pound of orange flowers a little while, and put them in, save the water and with that make a syrup to sweeten it."

Imagine a large 18th-century still with its boiler and the condensing chamber joined by long spiralling tubes. Here the cordial waters were made, sweetened with sugar and then later taken as a health-giving drink. These two recipes describe in detail how the cordials were made, the first using pot marigold flowers and saffron, the second using a whole collection of roses, rosemary, pinks, cowslips, borage and bugloss flowers. Flower syrups were often added to the cordials to cheer the heart or otherwise make a pleasant-tasting drink.

To make "The Saffron Cordial" also from *The Compleat Housewife*:

Fill a large still with marigold flowers, adding to them of nutmegs, mace, and English Saffron, of each an ounce: then take three pints of muscadine, or Malaga sack, and with a sprig of rosemary dash it on the flowers; then distil it off with a slow fire, and let it drop on white sugar candy, draw it off until it begins to be sour; save a pint of the first running to mix with the other waters on an extraordinary occasion, mix the rest together to drink it by itself. This Cordial is excellent in fainting and for the small pox or ague; take five or six spoonfuls at a time.

To make "Dr. Butler's Cordial Water against melancholy, etc. Most Approved" (from *The Queen's Closet Opened*, 1655):

Take the flowers of cowslips, Marigolds, Pinks, Clove, gillyflowers, single stock gillyflowers, of each four handfuls, the flowers of Rosemary, Damask Roses, of each three handfuls, Borage and Bugloss flowers, and Balm leaves, of each two handfuls, put them in a quart of Canary wine into a great bottle

Above: *Lavender flowers were an ingredient in many infusions and are still used in the kitchen today.*

Right: *Rosemary flowers form the basis of many refreshing tonics, and were recorded in recipes as early as the 17th century.*

or judge close stopped with a cork, sometimes stirring the flowers and wine together, adding to them Anniseeds bruised one dram, two nutmegs sliced, English Saffron two pennyworth; after some time infusion, distil them in a cold still with a hot fire, hanging at the nose of the Still Ambergreece [wax-like substance] and Musk, of each one grain, then to the distilled water put white sugar candy finely beaten six ounces, and put the glass wherein they are, into hot water for one hour. Take this water at one time three spoonfuls thrice a week, or when you are ill. It cureth all Melancholy fumes, and infinitely comforts the spirits.

Left: *Pot marigolds were a popular culinary flower, for their colour, flavour and supposed health-giving qualities.*

floral salads

One of the most exciting ways that flowers were used for the table was as a "strewing" flower on salads. In the 17th century, salads were greatly esteemed and many recipes have been recorded in minute detail.

It has been recorded that King James II's head gardener thought that there should be at least 35 ingredients in an ordinary salad. Quite a few roots would be used, such as elecampagne, daisy, fennel, angelica, rampion, parsnip and carrot and they were often candied, blanched, or boiled and then simply added when cold or pickled. The greenery was made up of sowthistle leaves, young spinach, young primrose and violet leaves, tarragon and rocket (arugula) leaves, the tops of red sage, hyssop, thyme, pot marigold and marjoram, lettuce, young mallow leaves, salad burnet, purslane, cowslip leaves, cress, young basil, borage and bugloss leaves, chervil, samphire, plantain and yarrow, vine tendrils, wood sorrel and very finely shredded young cabbage leaves. Ash keys, broom and elder buds were pickled and added and sometimes the candied buds of flowers were also mixed in. The salads were then dressed in an oil and vinegar mixture to which might be added dry grated mustard and the yolks of newly laid eggs.

Some of the salads were grand affairs, the very centre of a great feast or banquet. Some might have elaborately carved root vegetables, such as turnips, as a centrepiece. Intricately carved castles were popular designs. Records relate that the turnip castle would have been covered with rye paste and washed over with egg yolk, topped by a tree made in the same manner as the castle. In summer the tree would be green and hung with paste fruit and flowers. In winter it would be white, to resemble snow. In spring the castle might have steps leading up to a cross in recognition of Easter. The castle would sit on a mount with ramparts or rings below, where the salads would be laid out in various dishes. The castle might have four balconies where there might be four

Above: *Hibiscus and nasturtium flowers have been used in cooking for centuries. 17th-century documents relate that nasturtium buds were pickled for use in winter salads for grand banquets.*

statues of the four seasons. Each statue would hold a glass cruet of oil and vinegar in both hands. When all the guests were seated, the "Grand Sallet", as this impressive dish was called, was carried in, and set on a large table. Then the cruets were unstopped and the contents allowed to run over all the salads.

Summer or winter flowers were an integral part of such salads. Mention is often made of cowslip buds, flowers of borage and clove gillyflowers, broom buds, petals of violets, primroses, rosemary, nasturtium and pot marigold. Spring and summer "strewing" of these edible flowers must have been wonderful to see. In the middle of winter, fresh flowers would not be available, so the salads were presented with flowers preserved in vinegar or candied in sugar with savoury pickles and sweet candied flowers presented sitting side by side. The best wine vinegar was used to make an infusion of clove gillyflowers, roses, rosemary and nasturtiums. Borage, cowslips, pot marigolds, roses, violets and primroses were all candied.

Left: *One of the best-known of all the edible flowers, nasturtiums are still a popular salad flower, with the petals and buds imparting a peppery taste.*

The winter array was quite different in taste and texture to the spring and summer affairs as many of the ingredients had to be pickled or preserved in some way, but what a rich variety of flavours our ancestors still managed to enjoy.

John Evelyn, author of *Acetaria* (1699), records the name of a special winter salad recipe as being "Sallet-All-Sorts":

The Almonds blanch'd in cold water, cut them round and thin and so leave then in cold water. Then have pickled Cucumbers, Olives, Capers, Berberries, Red-Beet, Buds of Nasturtium, Broom etc., Purslan stalk, Sampier, Ash Keys, Walnuts, Mushrooms, with raisins of the Sun ston'd, citron and orange peel. Strew them over with any candy'd flowers and so dispose of them in the same Dish both mixt and by themselves. To these add Marrows, Pine kernels and of Almonds four times as much of the rest with some Rose-water. Here also come in the Pickled Flowers and Vinegar in little china Dishes. And thus you have an universal winter Sallet or an All sort in

compendium fitted for a City Feast and distinguished from the grand Sallet which should consist of the green blanched and unpickled under a stately Pennash of Sellery adorn'd with Buds and Flowers.

It was John Evelyn who provided a detailed description of how to pickle flowers. In *Acetaria* he wrote:

To Pickle Broom-Buds And Pods make a strong pickle of White Wine, Vinegar and Salt able to bear an Egg. Stir very well till the Salt be quite dissolved, clearing off the Dregs and Scum. The next day pour it from the Bottom, and having rubbed the Buds dry, pot them up in a pickle Glass, which should be frequently shaken till they sink under it, and keep it well stopt and covered. Thus may you pickle any other Buds.

Below: A 16th-century depiction of a hunting banquet includes fresh flowers decorating the food and table.

popular flowers in the past

There is no doubt that in the past, flowers were used regularly and often as part of everyday life in the kitchen. Of all the flowers that were used in the 16th and 17th centuries, violets, roses, rosemary, gillyflower, lavender and cowslips were among the most popular. It is fascinating to see just how many recipes were available for any one of these flowers, but cowslips particularly so.

Cowslips, which are now endangered, once grew in large quantities in grasslands and meadows. The cowslip flowers, or "pips" as they were often known, smelt of honey and were a favourite flower to be picked and used in springtime. Explicit instructions were given in a *Book of Fruit and Flowers* dated 1653, to pick them in the midst of the day when the dew has left them. Then the gatherer was told to "pull them out of the podds, and cut off the green Knobs at the lower end." It was good advice. By following this example, the flowers would be picked dry, but before the heat of the day had time to evaporate the essential oils. This technique still holds true today when gathering flowers.

Cowslip flowers were often strewn on salads along with the young leaves, but in order to preserve them for later use, especially in winter when there was a shortage of flowers and fresh greenery, cowslips were pickled. John Evelyn's recipe in 1699 suggests that to every pound of flowers, allow a pound of sugar and one pint of white wine vinegar. Bring the liquid to a boil until it is like a syrup, and then when scalding hot, pour it over the cowslip flowers. It sounds easy enough until you consider the vast quantities of flowers required for such a recipe: even a bucket of flowers weighs very little.

Cowslip flowers were also candied, sometimes in large bunches. Mrs Mary Eales, confectioner to Queen Anne, recorded the following procedure in 1719. First they were steeped in gum arabic, shaken and dried off, then dipped in fine sugar and hung to dry on a long string hung in front of the fire where they stayed for two or three days until the flowers were dry. What a lovely sight they must have been, along with all the other spring confections.

Sometimes a syrup of cowslips was made using distilled water and sugar. Three pounds of fresh blossoms were used to five pints of boiling water, and then simmered with sugar to a syrup.

Cowslip cream was made using a handful or two of both flowers and buds, bruised in a mortar, and boiled with a quart of cream. This was then seasoned with mace, and sugar and orange-flower water were added. The liquid was strained and then mixed with two egg yolks and another handful of flowers, only this time the cowslip "tops" or knobs had been clipped off. This rich creamy custard was recommended by Joseph Cooper, cook to Charles I, in his receipt book dated 1654.

Cowslips were often mentioned in recipes by royal cooks. Patrick Lamb, Head Cook successively to Charles II, James II, William and Mary, and Anne, records in his receipt book of 1716 a recipe for a cowslip tart using the blossoms of a gallon of cowslips, "minced exceedingly small" and mixed with grated Naples biscuit, one and a half pints of cream, eight eggs, sugar, rose-water and salt. It was then baked. A later adaptation of this was to put a ring of puff pastry around the top of the pie dish and pour the pudding inside.

One of the best-loved treats was cowslip wine. E.G. Hayden records in *Travels Round our Village* how one quart of cowslips would be used with nine pints of water, two pounds of sugar and two spoonfuls of yeast. He mentioned that it would keep for a year but one wonders whether there would be any left

Left: *Scented violets were a particular favourite in Victorian times, when they were crystallized and used as a decoration on desserts or chocolates, or made into candies.*

Above: *In the past cowslips had many uses in the kitchen, and were often picked and used in salads, puddings and cakes. They were even enjoyed as sweets or in wine.*

Above: *Primroses were another well-loved culinary flower. They would typically be crystallized or preserved to be used in the winter months.*

when the meadows were next in bloom. Sometimes oranges and lemons were added to cowslip wine, while cowslip mead was also made using honey, sweet briar and lemon for extra flavouring.

Cowslip wine remained popular right up to the early part of the 20th century and was one of the few flower wines mentioned by Mrs Beeton in the various editions of her mammoth book, *Household Management*, first published in 1861. Recipes for clary and dandelion flower wines were included in some editions, along with instructions for making a hawthorn flower liqueur.

By the 1920s, updated editions of *Household Management* included only those flower wines listed above, out of a total of 35 wine recipes including exotics such as orange, lemon, ginger, peach, and apricot, as well as more homely brews such as apple, damson and gooseberry. Elderberry wine was included, but not elderflower champagne. Popular wine recipes of the 16th and 17th centuries, including

meadowsweet, broom, clover, lime blossom, fennel, golden rod, hawthorn blossom, mint, primrose and tansy, had all but disappeared from mainstream cookbooks by the second half of the 19th century.

No recipes for flower pickles were mentioned by Mrs Beeton, although plenty of fruit pickles were listed including a recipe for Indian mango chutney. There was nothing on preserving or crystallizing flowers although there were many recipes for crystallizing fruit such as greengages, cherries and apricots. In over 1600 pages of *Household Management* not one reference to flower syrups or flower vinegars is to be found. Nasturtiums make a brief appearance as a salad ingredient, but their main use is for the seeds to be pickled, like capers. By the 1920s, most references to culinary flowers were dropped. Eleanour Sinclair Rohde seems a lone voice in her book *A Garden of Herbs* published in 1920 and it has taken almost 80 years to revive and reshape the old ideas for use at the dining tables of today.

Using Flowers

Flowers can be used in the kitchen in so many varied and glorious ways – as colourful butters, scented oils, aromatic vinegars and delicious sugars. With the addition of egg white and sugar, they are transformed into crystallized flowers and can grace any cakes, cookies, mousses or roulades. Fresh flowers have a lot to offer today's cook. This chapter includes ideas from savoury to sweet.

Right: Roses and lavender have long been prized in the kitchen as well as the garden.

Gathering Flowers

Flowers should be gathered on a warm dry morning, before the sun has become too strong and drawn out the essential oils. They are best picked in bud or freshly opened, when their scent and flavour are at their most enticing. When picking flowers for culinary purposes, they should be organically home-grown. If you use plants from nurseries or garden centres, ensure the plants have not been treated with pesticides.

Ignore dusty or dirty flowers from the roadside and avoid any that have been sprayed with insecticide. Never pick old flowers that have lost their freshness, scent and flavour.

Those who are allergic to pollen should not eat flowers. In any case, it is still best to cut out the central reproductive areas, where the stamens and pollen are to be found, if you can. Individual flowers vary a great deal but some flowers, such as lilies, hibiscus and hollyhocks, are particularly heavy with pollen and it is obvious which parts should be removed. With smaller flowers such as primroses, violets, cowslips, violas, sage, chives, marjoram and basil this would be difficult in the extreme, so if anyone is susceptible to allergy it is best to avoid all flowers.

Remove any green parts surrounding the flowers. This includes the stem and the calyx. The calyx is the whorl of sepals which sits at the top of the stem just below the petals. It is obvious on some flowers and not on others. Primroses, cowslips, daisies, borage, anchusa and sage are all easily pulled away from the calyx, leaving the petals joined and intact. Violas and violets are slightly more difficult and you might end up with individual petals. From a culinary point of view, this

Above: *Hollyhocks provide a wealth of edible petals throughout late summer.*

doesn't matter since they are the important part. With some flowers such as roses and hollyhocks, the calyx cannot be pulled off and so it is easier to simply cut or pull off the petals. With pot marigolds, daisies and sunflowers the petals are easily pulled away individually or in small groups.

Many flowers formed in the shape of flat or rounded umbels, such as fennel, dill, sweet cicely, chives and angelica, do not have this green calyx at their base. Simply remove the tiny stems as far as possible and use the flowers whole. Roses and alpine pinks have a bitter white heel at the base of the petal, which is best removed.

Above: *Marigold petals can be pulled away easily.*

Above: *Chive flowers can be snipped off the main stem.*

WARNING

You are encouraged to grow rather than pick the flowers. Do not pick wild flowers that are endangered, such as cowslips; these can be cultivated from seed. This book lists those flowers which are commonly edible (see Plant Directory). However, the list is not exhaustive. Meanwhile, there are plenty of flowers around the world which are most definitely not safe to eat such as Euphorbia, Rhododendron, Anemone, Aquilegia, Helleborus, Hedera, Wisteria and Laburnum, to name a few. If in any doubt, do NOT eat them. Stick to those listed in the Plant Directory where there are plenty of glorious, pretty and tasty flowers which are safe to use and are perfectly delicious. Moreover, they have been tried and tested for generations.

preparing pollen-heavy flowers

Hollyhocks are available in many different colours from yellow to pale pink and rich maroon. The flowers are sometimes single, sometimes double. They are all edible.

1 △ *Pick the flower on a warm dry morning. Choose one that is freshly opened with no bees feasting on the pollen.*

2 △ *Cut out the central reproductive organs which will be heavy with pollen.*

3 △ *Brush any excess pollen off the petals using a fine brush.*

4 △ *Cut away any green parts at the base of the flowers. Remove any small pieces that remain stuck to the petals.*

5 ◁ *You are left with the petals only. These can be used in either fruit or green salads.*

getting rid of insects

Spring and early summer flowers are usually free from winged visitors, but by mid-summer insects are far more often in evidence. For obvious reasons, take care not to pick a flower with a bee clinging to it.

USING SALT WATER

1 ◁ *Elderflowers seem to attract tiny insects and often the easiest way to get rid of them is to dip them into salted water. Prepare a bowl with some cold water and add a spoonful of salt, then stir.*

2 ◁ *Dip the flowers into the salted water and gently move them around. Remove the flowers, give them a gentle shake and pat them dry with kitchen paper.*

FEIGNING NIGHT-TIME

If you find tiny rape or pollen beetles in the base of the flowers, pick the flowers and gently shake them to remove the insects. If any remain, put the flowers in a dark environment and the beetles will leave in search of light.

1 ◁ *Place the flowers in water and cover them with a brown envelope. Then put them in a dark corner, preferably the potting shed. The little beetles will fall off the flower and try to escape to the light. They are not harmful – just a nuisance.*

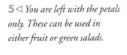

Floral Butters

Floral butters are a delightful and easy way to preserve flowers and a marvellous way to use them in the kitchen. Kept in a sealed container in the refrigerator, they will keep for two weeks or more, while in the freezer they can be kept for three months. Not only do floral butters look and taste good but they are extremely versatile.

Savoury butters may be used to spread on open sandwiches, bagels, rolls or toast. Try chive-flower butter with egg toppings, dill-flower butter with salmon, or sage-flower butter with pâtés or frankfurters. You could spread them on crusty bread or crackers and eat with cheese. They are also excellent served with fresh vegetables. Try mint-flower butter with fresh new potatoes, or thyme-flower butter with steamed baby carrots.

Sweet floral butters are just as delicious, if not more so, but their uses are quite different. A handful of highly scented rose petals mixed with butter and icing (confectioners') sugar will transform an ordinary layer cake into something very memorable. A wonderful combination is the purple rose 'William Lobb' mixed with the rich pink rose 'Gertrude Jekyll'. The resulting mixture is speckled with purple and pink flecks of rose petals and tastes wonderful. There are a great many highly scented roses which would be equally good. It is a

Above: *A mixture of rose petals including purple 'William Lobb' and pink 'Gertrude Jekyll'. Together they make an excellent combination for a rose-petal butter cream.*

question of experimenting to find your favourites. You don't have to stick with just one kind of flower, either. Try a combination of violets and primroses to make butter icing (frosting) for a Mother's Day cake.

Above: *Chives.*

Right and far right: *Sage and thyme flowers are wonderful additions to savoury butters.*

FLORAL BUTTER BALLS

This technique can be used with any of the savoury flowers. Where large petals are used, such as pot marigolds, you may prefer to snip them smaller.

- SERVES 6–8 people to accompany vegetables
- INGREDIENTS
  30ml/2 tbsp flowers; thyme flowers were used here

  50g/2oz unsalted butter, softened

1 △ *Remove the individual thyme florets or flowers from the flower-head and mix with softened butter.*

2 △ *Make little patty shapes by using two wooden butter boards or spoons. Refrigerate in a sealed container until ready to use.*

3 △ *Place thyme butter balls on top of steaming carrots and serve immediately. Or use as a topping for grilled tomatoes or* *mushrooms. Any excess butter can be kept in the refrigerator for up to 2 weeks or frozen for up to 3 months.*

MIXED-FLOWER BUTTER DISH

Here, sage and chive flowers are combined to form layers of flowers between unsalted butter but you can use any of the flowers suggested opposite. Left for 24 hours, the flavour of the flowers impregnates the butter and creates a visual centre-piece for the table.

- MAKES 115g/4oz
- INGREDIENTS
  60ml/4 tbsp flowers; sage and chives were used here

  115g/4oz unsalted butter

1 △ *Pull the sage flowers away from the stems. Cut the chives off the flower-heads. Place a layer of chive and sage flowers in the middle of a dish. Place half the butter over the flowers. Add more flowers on top.*

2 △ *Add the second half of butter over the middle layer and press down gently to create a good seal. Then press additional flowers around the four sides.*

3 △ *Finally, scatter more flowers over the top of the butter if you wish. Cover and refrigerate for 24 hours before use. Use to butter rolls to accompany a chilled summer* *soup, a tasty onion tart or a strong flavoured pâté. The butter can be kept in the refrigerator for up to 2 weeks or frozen for up to 3 months.*

ROSE-PETAL BUTTER

This method combines sweetly scented petals with butter and icing (confectioners') sugar to create a sweet filling to sandwich between two layers of a Victoria sponge cake. The flavour is superb and will certainly be noticed and appreciated by all who taste it. The more scented the petals, the better the flavour. Choose newly opened flowers and pick on a dry morning.

- MAKES ENOUGH TO FILL A
  20CM/8IN CAKE
- INGREDIENTS
  60ml/4 tbsp sweetly
  scented petals

  115g/4oz butter, softened
  115g/4oz icing
  (confectioners') sugar

1 △ *Separate the rose petals from the flower-head. Remove the white heel at the base of the rose petals and chop the petals finely. Use a mixture of different petals if you prefer.*

2 △ *Beat the softened butter with a wooden spoon or an electric mixer until it has become very creamy in colour. Add the icing sugar, a little at a time, and the rose petals.*

3 △ *Spread between two halves of a Victoria sponge cake, or other light layer cake, or use as butter icing (frosting) in fairy (cup) cakes. Any leftover mixture can be covered with*

cling film (plastic wrap) and kept in the refrigerator for up to 2 weeks or frozen for up to 3 months.

ICED ROSE-PETAL CAKE

- SERVE 10–12
- INGREDIENTS
  For the cake
  225g/8oz butter or
    margarine, softened
  225g/8oz caster (superfine)
    sugar
  4 medium eggs
  225g/8oz self-raising
    (self-rising) flour

  5ml/1tsp baking powder
  For the filling
  1 quantity rose-petal butter

- TO FINISH
  225g/8oz icing
    (confectioners') sugar
  30–45ml/2–3tbsp rose-water
  6–8 pink roses, and several
    rose petals, crystallized

> **COOK'S TIP**
> Alpine pinks could also be used to make a sweet butter. Choose the most scented varieties and use individual petals (remove white heel). The whole flowers can be crystallized in the same way as for the rose petals.

1 *Preheat the oven to 180ºC/350ºF/Gas 4. Grease and line the bases of two 20cm/8in round sandwich tins (pans). Put the cake ingredients in a large bowl and beat until light and creamy. Divide between the prepared tins and level the surfaces. Bake for about 25 minutes until just firm to the touch. Transfer to a wire rack to cool.*

2 *Sandwich the cake together on a serving plate with the rose-petal butter mix.*

3 *Beat the icing sugar in a bowl with 30ml/2 tbsp of the rose-water to give a consistency that thickly coats the back of a spoon. Add more rose-water, drop by drop, if necessary.*

4 *Spoon the icing over the cake, allowing the icing to run down the sides in places. Decorate with a circle of crystallized roses and petals.*

Right: *A glorious rose-petal cake complete with crystallized roses.*

Floral Oils

Unlike many other foods these days, flowers have only a short season of availability and so need to be preserved in some way if they are to be enjoyed once the season is past. One of the best ways to preserve their special flavour is to make floral oils. They will last from three to six months and will give you a chance to savour many of the unique flavours long after the flowers have disappeared. Floral oils don't take long to prepare, and they are a very easy way of making the most of a bumper crop of flowers such as marjoram or lavender.

For sweeter flowers such as lavender, cowslips, or rose petals it is probably best to use a light sunflower oil. For the hearty flavours of hyssop, fennel, dill, mint, marjoram, thyme and basil use olive oil, or you might like to try walnut or even hazelnut oil. The results will be very different but worth the experiment.

Many of the floral oils can be used to enhance particular kinds of dishes – lavender or hyssop oil may be used to sear chicken before cooking it in a casserole. Fennel or dill oil could be used to fry fish; sage oil might be used to baste pork or turkey. Marjoram or lavender oil both work well drizzled over a pizza just before it goes in the oven. Try thyme oil with tomatoes or mushrooms before roasting. Or use thyme, pot marigold or marjoram oil as a dressing on pasta. Mint, salad rocket (arugula) or violet oil would all make wonderful

Above: *Make marjoram-flower oil in late summer when blossoms are plentiful.*

additions to a vinaigrette, and will all result in remarkably different flavours. It is also possible to make oil from roses and rosemary flowers. The list of flavours is almost endless.

Left: *Richly flavoured lavender-flower oil adds a wonderful flavour to any pizza.*

Right: *Purple basil flowers can be preserved in oil to enjoy during the winter months.*

MARJORAM-FLOWER OIL

This wonderfully fragrant oil is very simple to make and can be used in so many different ways. Mix it with breadcrumbs and garlic to top baked mushrooms, tomatoes or (bell) peppers, or use it to cook an aromatic omelette.

- MAKES 450ML/¾PINT/2 CUPS
- INGREDIENTS
  30–40 flower clusters, clean, dry and free of insects

450ml/¾pint/2 cups olive oil
(not extra virgin)

1 △ *Fill a jam jar with lots of marjoram flower heads. It is not necessary to remove the flowers individually. It will not matter if you include leaves.*

2 △ *Cover completely with the olive oil. It is important that the oil covers the flowers – any that are not covered will go mouldy. Place the jar on a sunny window-sill for one month. Shake the jar occasionally.*

3 △ *Strain the oil into a jug (pitcher) through a piece of muslin (cheesecloth) or clean coffee filter.*

4 △ *Pour the strained liquid into a pretty bottle and add a complete flower or some petals to decorate. The oil will keep for 3 months if extra flowers have been added, or 6 months without extra flowers.*

COOK'S TIP

Marjoram blooms over a period of several weeks in late summer, producing a huge quantity of flowers, so you may like to make more than one jar.

Sweet Flowers

Crystallizing flower petals is a simple and very effective way of preserving them for future use, and the sugar enhances their delicate flavour. The results can also look spectacular. This is particularly true of primroses, violets, cowslips, alpine pinks and roses, but there is a wide range to choose from and they are all beautiful. Try bright blue anchusa, starry-petalled borage or vivid-red pineapple sage. Use them individually or try different combinations to create a masterpiece.

Some flowers, such as primroses, cowslips, borage, sage and anchusa, are easy to pull away from their green calyx and can be crystallized whole. Daisies, roses and pinks are often best divided into individual petals, although you might consider treating the entire flower head for a real showpiece.

Above: The crystallized violas are complemented by variegated mint leaves.

CRYSTALLIZING FLOWERS

• INGREDIENTS
1 egg white
50g/2oz caster (superfine)
    sugar
lots of individual petals
    and/or entire flowers

1 △ A simple way to crystallize flowers is to use egg white and caster sugar, but they will only last up to 2 days. First gather your flowers when they are dry. Take each petal individually or the flower as a whole, depending on the effect you want to achieve. Place the egg white and sugar in separate saucers.

2 △ To crystallize petals, take each individual petal or whole flower-head and paint the petals both front and back with the egg white.

3 △ Lightly cover both sides with caster sugar. You will find that it sticks to the damp surface.

COOK'S TIP
When using either roses or alpine pinks, be sure to remove the white heel at the base of the petal, which has a bitter taste.

WARNING
Raw eggs should not be consumed by pregnant women, babies, young children or the elderly. If in doubt, substitute powdered egg white.

Above: A variety of roses has been crystallized whole, making a visual feast on top of a rose-petal layer cake.

4 △ *Lay inidvidual petals on a sheet of parchment paper and keep them in a warm, dry place overnight, or until crisp. Store in a sealed container until needed. Petals crystallized in this way should last up to 2 days.*

5 △ *After treating whole flower-heads, attach a piece of thread to the base of the flower or push florist's wire through the base. Drape the heads around a glass by attaching the thread with tape or bending the wires. Allow to dry as for the individual petals.*

LONGER-LASTING CRYSTALLIZATION

You can use gum arabic instead of egg white to coat the petals before treating with caster (superfine) sugar and drying in the manner described opposite. This method allows the petals to stay fresh for several months rather than days. Buy the gum arabic from a chemist and dissolve 5ml/1 tsp in 25ml/1½ tbsp water or a colourless spirit (alcohol) such as gin or vodka.

Above: Crystallized roses make an exquisite decoration for rose-petal sorbet.

FLORAL SUGAR

This is an easy but effective method of capturing the flavour of sweet flowers. Many different types can be made, including violet, pink, citrus flower, rose, lavender and also mint. The stronger the scent, the more tasty the results.

- MAKES 225G/8OZ/2 CUPS
- INGREDIENTS

  225g/8oz/2 cups icing
  (confectioners'), caster

  (superfine) or granulated
  (white) sugar

  90–180ml/6–12tbsp whole
  or chopped flower petals

1 Place the sugar and petals into a food processor and blend. Store in a sealed container for a week.

2 Sift the sugar to remove the flower petals and put the sugar into a jar or another airtight container. Use it to make butter-cream fillings for cakes, and to add flavour to meringues and sorbets.

Right: *Meringues can be made with rose-petal sugar, decorated with crystallized alpine pinks.*

ALMOND FLOWER COOKIES

- MAKES ABOUT 24
- INGREDIENTS

  115g/4oz butter
  115g/4oz caster (superfine)
  sugar
  115g/4oz ground almonds
  1 egg, separated
  5ml/1 tsp vanilla extract
  115g/4oz plain (all-purpose)
  flour, sifted

- TO DECORATE

  75–100 crystallized alpine
  pink petals (rose petals,
  primroses or violets could
  also be used)
  Icing to secure flowers (50g/
  2oz icing (confectioners')
  sugar mixed with 7.5ml/
  1½ tsp water)

1 Preheat the oven to 180ºC/350ºF/Gas 4. Grease a baking sheet.

2 In a large bowl, beat together the butter and sugar until light and fluffy. Add the ground almonds, egg yolk, vanilla extract and flour and then knead the mixture until blended.

3 Roll the dough into small balls about 2.5cm/1in diameter, then place on the baking sheet. Brush with slightly beaten egg white and bake for about 15 minutes. Cool the cookies on a wire rack.

4 To decorate the cookies, secure crystallized alpine pink petals on the top with a little icing.

Opposite: *Almond flower cookies with a floral topping.*

Left: *Flower-scented sugar can be sprinkled over yogurt or cream.*

Hot Drinks and Tisanes

Flower teas are known as "tisanes" and offer a very quick, cheap and easy way of enjoying a refreshing drink. Many of them can be enjoyed hot or cold depending on personal preference or the time of day. Lemon or honey may be added for extra flavour or sweetness, but avoid milk. These are light and fragrant teas and should be kept very clean and clear.

Many flowers are suitable, such as chamomile, dandelion, elderflower, hyssop, rose petal, dill flower, lemon verbena, lavender, lime blossom, jasmine, peppermint, bergamot and hibiscus as well as many others. Just take a small quantity of clean flowers (and in the case of lemon verbena, peppermint and bergamot you can add a few leaves as well) and add a cup of boiling water. Allow to infuse for about four minutes, then remove the flowers and foliage if used. Drink either warm or chilled. Many of these flowers can be dried and used on a later occasion. Dry them in the shade and keep them in labelled airtight tins.

Many herbal teas have been used for medicinal purposes for centuries. Lavender, hyssop, thyme and marjoram were all taken to alleviate cold symptoms, while hops, chamomile and lime flower were used against insomnia. Whatever the virtues, the scent of these tisanes alone is a tonic and they can be enjoyed simply for this reason.

Above: Lavender tisane.

HYSSOP TISANE

Put one sprig of flowering hyssop in a cup and add boiling water. In 4 minutes, remove the flower and enjoy a remarkable tisane which is very pleasantly flavoured and a beautiful pale aquamarine in colour. Drink it either hot or cold. It is thought to be helpful in alleviating the symptoms of colds and sore throats.

LEMON VERBENA TISANE

Take off a flowering spray of lemon verbena and a couple of leaves and put it all in a cup. Add boiling water and allow to infuse for 4 minutes. Remove the flowers and foliage and enjoy a warm, lemon-flavoured drink which is pale golden in colour and wonderfully refreshing. You could add a little honey for extra flavour and sweetness, or allow it to go cold and drink chilled.

LAVENDER TISANE

Place two or three sprigs of lavender flowers in a glass cup and pour boiling water over. Allow to infuse for about 4 minutes before removing the lavender flowers. The tisane will have turned pale blue in colour, with an uplifting lavender scent.

BERGAMOT TISANE

The Oswegan Indians of North America made tea from bergamot leaves. After the Boston Tea Party in 1773 colonial settlers adopted the practice as a tea substitute. The flowers have the same flavour as the leaves but they are sweeter and far more flamboyant. Make the drink by pouring hot water onto a head of bergamot mixed with 2.5ml/½ tsp of orange pekoe tea. Allow to infuse, strain and then float some fresh petals on top.

Right: *Lime-blossom tisane. Like chamomile tea, tisanes made with lime blossom can induce a good night's sleep.*

Below left: *Chamomile tisane.*

Below right: *Hibiscus and rosemary tisane.*

CHAMOMILE TISANE

Chamomile flowers provide one of the best known sedative teas, which, like lime blossom, is meant to help induce a gentle sleep. The tisane can be rather bitter if you use too many flowers or infuse for too long. Try it with three or four flower-heads only and add a little honey if you wish. The fragrance is powerful and very attractive.

LIME BLOSSOM TISANE

Pick lime flowers when they begin to open. Use five or six fresh lime flowers for each cup and add hot, but not boiling, water. Steep for no longer than 3–4 minutes, then strain. It can be drunk either hot or cold, with a slice of lemon or sweetened with honey if necessary. It is a pale lemon colour and tastes surprisingly creamy.

HIBISCUS AND ROSEMARY TISANE

Hibiscus flowers look flamboyant and exotic with their exquisite colouring and wide papery petals. The flavour on its own can be disappointing so combine it with a sprig of rosemary. Add boiling water, and after 4 minutes, remove the rosemary but leave the hibiscus in place. The result is very pleasing; a fragrant, tasty tisane with an exotic flower to peer into every time you sip. You could drink it chilled and add a new flower.

PEPPERMINT TISANE

Just one sprig of leaves and flowers is enough to flavour a delicious tisane which has lots of peppermint flavour without being overpowering. Hot or cold, this is definitely one to try.

Cold Drinks, Punches and Cordials

Many cold drinks, both alcoholic and non-alcoholic, are flavoured with flowers. Sparkling elderflower and elderflower cordial are perhaps two of the best known. Both are equally delicious, with sparkling elderflower adding a real sense of occasion. Recipes still exist for many drinks that few of us drink nowadays.

Flowers from the fields and commonlands such as primrose, clary sage, clover, meadowsweet, broom and gorze were all harvested to make wine in season, while those from the hedgerows included hawthorn blossom and honeysuckle. Chamomile and lime blossoms were used to make tea and wine. Different liqueurs were flavoured with violets, hawthorn and angelica. Dandelions and hops were brewed into both wine and beer, while hops and cowslips were also combined with honey to make mead.

Sweet woodruff has long been a popular ingredient in drinks. Native to many woodland areas of Europe, it is used in a variety of ways. In Germany chilled Moselle or other white wine is flavoured with sweet woodruff leaves and flowers and left to stand for half an hour. Then it is served in tankards with fresh sprigs of flowers and a slice of lemon. In France sweet woodruff is served with champagne and in Switzerland it is used to flavour Cognac and Benedictine. Woodruff can also be used to flavour apple juice, or mixed with strawberry leaves to make a tisane.

Above: It just would not be summer without a jug of refreshing punch. Here, mint flowers and leaves, and bright blue borage add the finishing touch.

SPARKLING ELDERFLOWER DRINK

Above: Elderflower.

- MAKES 4.5L/1 GALLON
- INGREDIENTS

600g/1¼lb granulated (white) sugar

4.5 litre/1 gallon water

6–8 large heads of young elderflowers, dry and free from insects

2 lemons, sliced

30ml/2 tbsp white wine vinegar

1 Dissolve the sugar in 2.25 litres/4 pints of hot (not boiling) water. Add a further 2.25litres/4 pints of cold water.

2 When cool add the elderflowers, sliced lemons and white wine vinegar and then leave to stand for 24–48 hours.

3 Strain into strong glass bottles and cork tightly. (It might be safer to use wires to hold down the tops.) The drink will be ready to serve in about 6 days.

MINT-FLOWER YOGURT DRINK

Enjoy this thick, fruity drink on a hot summer's day. Fresh peaches could be substituted for the raspberries.

- SERVES 2
- INGREDIENTS

225ml/8fl oz/1 cup natural (plain) yogurt
100ml/4fl oz/½ cup mineral water
75g/3oz raspberries

50g/2oz sugar
2 sprigs flowering mint

- TO DECORATE
2 sprigs flowering mint

1 ◁ *Place all the ingredients in a food processor and purée. Pour the mixture into a glass jug and chill.*

2 ▷ *Serve in tall glasses, each decorated with a sprig of mint flowers.*

ROSE-PETAL AND STRAWBERRY PUNCH

This makes a memorable party piece with its colourful petals and deep pink colour. Use raspberries instead of strawberries if you prefer.

- SERVES 8–10
- INGREDIENTS

1 bottle of rosé wine, chilled
60ml/4 tbsp vodka
75g/3oz strawberries, sliced

handful of scented rose petals, white heels at the base removed
1 bottle of carbonated mineral water

1 ◁ *Pour the chilled bottle of rosé wine into a glass punch bowl. Add the vodka and sliced strawberries.*

2 ▷ *Scatter a handful of scented rose petals on top. Chill for 1 hour. Add the bottle of carbonated mineral water before serving.*

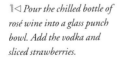

Frozen Flowers

Nothing could be more attractive than preserving flowers in ice. You can use floral ice cubes to cool your summer drinks such as lemonade and punch, or use them as the centrepiece in a chilled soup. For a party or other occasion, make a dramatic display of frozen flowers preserved in an ice bowl.

The ice bowl could contain a chilled punch, sorbet or other dessert, again, flavoured with petals. This is rather more time-consuming, but certainly worth the extra effort. There are many flowers to choose from, including all varieties of scented geraniums, miniature roses, borage, alpine pinks, sweet rocket and mints. Choose flowers for their dramatic shape and colour or for the exquisite markings on the petals. The results can be stunning.

FLORAL ICE CUBES

The process for making these pretty ice cubes is easy, but first you must judge the shapes and size of the individual flowers you want to freeze compared with the size of the compartments of the ice tray. In the case of scented geraniums, for example, the whole flower-head is much too big for an individual ice cube. Use just one or two florets as the proportions will be much better for most ice trays. Remember to remove as much of the stem and green parts as possible while still allowing the floret to stay together.

COOK'S TIP
The ice cubes don't have to be made with water – you can use lemonade or fruit juice. The contrast of fruit and flower adds a delicious flavour to your drink as the ice melts.

Above: An ice-cube tray of frozen scented geraniums.

Right: All edible flowers can be preserved in ice and will make any drink extra special.

- MAKES 2 TRAYS
- INGREDIENTS
  A selection of fresh, clean flowers
  water to fill 2 ice trays

1 *First prepare the flowers. Snip the florets off scented geraniums. You may get as many as four or six from one flower-head. Use them individually or as little groups.*

2 △ *Pour water in the ice-cube tray, filling it about half full.*

3 △ *Place the florets or individual petals on top of the water using tweezers if preferred. Freeze.*

4 △ *Remove from the freezer and add more water to bring to the top of the ice-cube tray. Freeze until needed.*

FLORAL ICE BOWL

This is a very dramatic way to show off some of the most beautiful edible flowers. It means you can use large rose petals or even whole flowers. You don't have to use one type of flower or colour. Try combining cold blues and pinks together or different varieties of flowers with a few leaves.

It is only a matter of time before the ice bowl melts, no matter what the room temperature, so it is best to use it to serve ice creams and sorbets, chilled frosted fruit or other cold desserts. Put the bowl on a plate or cake stand which has been kept very cold in the refrigerator. When the dessert has have been served, the ice will slowly melt and the flowers will look even more ephemeral and beautiful in the process.

- MAKES 1 LARGE BOWL
- INGREDIENTS
  A selection of pink roses, buds and leaves
  12 small flowers such as violas, small alpine pinks or daisies
  ice cubes

1 △ *Scatter several roses, buds, small flowers and sprigs of leaves into the base of a large 3.1 litre/5½ pint bowl. Make sure that the flowers do not touch each other. Weigh them down with plenty of ice cubes.*

2 △ *Rest a 1.7 litre/3 pint bowl over the ice so that it sits in the centre, leaving an even space between the two bowls. Pour cold water between the bowls until the water comes about 4cm/1½in up the sides. If the smaller bowl starts to move around, tuck crumpled kitchen paper between the bowls so it remains in the centre. Put in the freezer and place weights in the centre bowl (kitchen weights are ideal).*

3 △ *Once frozen (about 2–3 hours) remove from the freezer and discard the weights. Tuck more flowers, petals and leaves between the bowls and top up to 5mm/¼in of the rim with water. Freeze for at least 5 hours or overnight until solid. Remove from the freezer and leave for 5 minutes. Fill a washing bowl with hot water and immerse the two round bowls for a few seconds. Invert onto a plate and lift away the outer bowl. You may need to immerse the bowls several times in order to loosen the outer bowl sufficiently, but don't leave the bowls in hot water for too long as the ice bowl will start to melt. To remove the centre bowl, turn it the right way up, pour some hot water into the centre and twist the bowl until it will lift out. Return the ice bowl to the freezer until ready to use.*

COOK'S TIP

Ice bowls make beautiful containers for ice cream and sorbet. You can make an ice bowl in any size you like, from individual serving bowls to very large containers. Whichever size you choose, make sure when making them that there is about 2cm/¾in between the glass bowls when one sits inside the other.

Right: *Here the ice bowl is used as an exquisite container to hold rose sorbet.*

Flowers for Salads

So many flowers make wonderful additions to salads and yet very few are actually used on a day-to-day basis. We are reasonably familiar with nasturtiums in salads, others might have tried chives, but how many have used the crunchy mangetouts (snow pea) flavour of day lilies or the punchy, nutty flavour of sweet rocket flowers to pep up a salad?

There are many different qualities inherent in salad flowers. First there is the matter of texture; some are silky smooth to eat, such as hollyhocks and evening primroses; others have a definite crunchy quality, such as day lilies and chives.

Second, there is flavour: there are those that taste of aniseed, such as sweet cicely and fennel. Some, such as nasturtiums, are hot and peppery, and others, such as salad rocket (arugula), are nutty. Borage tastes just like cucumber, while sage, thyme and marjoram taste like a sweeter version of their leaves. The same is true of the flowers of rosemary, basil and hyssop. As children, many of us may have sucked nectar from sweet white nettles and pink clover. Here, in many of the garden flowers, you will find the same delicious, sweet flavour at the base.

Colour is an additional benefit in using salad flowers. Their brilliant colours add greatly to our enjoyment of them and to their effect on a salad. Some are outstandingly bold – pot marigolds are available in a wide range of vibrant oranges and yellows. Nasturtiums and sunflowers share the same vibrancy and have many different shades of red. Day lilies also grow in

Above: *Pot marigolds and curried eggs.*

many different shades although the soft orange is probably the most common and certainly attractive. Anchusa is a brilliant, rich blue; hyssop and sage are almost as strong. Borage is a rather softer blue but particularly striking, with its central area of black stamens. Bergamot might be pink or red, while hollyhock might range from almost black to pale yellow or white. Primroses, cowslips, fennel and dill will provide yellow shades, but the best yellow of all is the evening primrose.

salad flowers through the seasons

In springtime, pale yellow primroses make a tasty and very pretty salad ingredient as do both purple and white scented violets. A scattering of any of these blooms will instantly transform a bed of lettuce. Use them sprinkled over hard-boiled eggs, cucumber or tomatoes. Slightly later, sweet-smelling cowslips and colourful pink, red or white double daisies can be used to equally good effect. Rosemary flowers are small, but very sweet and tasty and a very beautiful blue.

In late spring and early summer sweet cicely will be in flower. Its tiny lacy white blooms have a strong aniseed flavour which will add a distinctive and surprising taste to the simplest of salads. The leaves and, later, the semi-ripe seeds have the same flavourful quality and are just as welcome in the salad bowl. By then, chives are coming into flower with their lilac domes of pungent onion-flavoured florets. Cast over eggs or

Above: *Balti Salad*

lettuce, they make a very pretty addition and have a welcome crunchy quality to them. Soon sage is in bloom with a long succession of tasty tubular flowers. Pot marigolds will then be open with their generous numbers of petals. Every petal is packed with wonderful colour and is lovely to scatter over all types of salads, either alone or combined with chive flowers.

A favourite flower at this time is borage. Its exquisite combination of black and blue colouring, its delicate but determined shape and its sweet cucumber flavour are really superb. The flavour of the borage flower lends itself to both green and fruit salads. Anchusa has the same dual purpose. It may not be high on flavour, but its intense blue is wonderful to use and ideal set against a simple orange salad.

By early summer a wide variety of scented alpine pinks is in flower, so, too, scented geraniums and sweet rocket (arugula). Soon, tall hollyhocks and papery hibiscus will begin to unfurl their exquisite blooms. They will all certainly add great beauty to a salad, if less flavour than other flowers. If you crave both colour and flavour, try pineapple sage. Its graceful, tubular flowers are sweet and utterly delicious, and are quite spectacular in their brilliant red vestments. All of these can grace any summer fruit salad bowl, but there is nothing to stop them being used in green salads as well.

Salad rocket (arugula) might be open at this time, depending on the sowing time. Some gardeners throw it away if and when it runs to seed, but in the process it will have come into flower and as long as you remember to keep dead-heading it, the flowers will continue to appear. Salad rocket has a distinctly nutty taste. Its four petals create a shape like a Maltese Cross and although at first it might look insignificant compared to some of the more showy blooms, the reverse of the petals displays some beautiful veining.

Above: *Anchusa combines beautifully with fresh oranges.*

Later in the season, flowers such as pink or red bergamot, fiery coloured nasturtiums and sunflowers are excellent in leafy salads. Young bergamot and nasturtium leaves can be added for texture, shape and flavour. Slices of dark beetroot (beets) would look wonderful with all these vibrant colours. Yellow flowers of dill and fennel are always good with a salad or with fish or pâté. Basil flowers may be small, but they taste so deliciously sweet and aromatic that they should certainly be used wherever possible. A simple tomato salad will be transformed with basil flowers. Thyme and hyssop flowers are also small but they are colourful and tasty and should be used quite freely, especially with chicken. All the marjorams or oreganos have a warm, aromatic quality to the flowers. They can be used with confidence and will make a valuable addition to a pizza or salad. All the mints will flower, so use them to add interest to almost any green salad. In addition, mint flowers make a wonderful salad vinaigrette.

Above: *Hollyhocks and nectarines with mint flowers.*

Above: *A fruit plate of borage and summer berries.*

Above: *Evening primroses and fresh melon.*

EARLY SUMMER SALAD WITH SAGE AND CHIVE FLOWERS

- SERVES 4–6
- INGREDIENTS
  2 little gem lettuce heads
  100g/3½oz sugar snap peas
  ¼ cucumber
  2 sticks celery
  small handful each of sage
    and chive flowers, green
    parts removed

For the dressing
60ml/4 tbsp mild olive oil
10ml/2 tsp lemon juice
coarse salt and ground
  black pepper

1 *Separate the lettuce leaves and tear larger ones into smaller pieces. Halve the sugar snap peas lengthways. Halve and thinly slice the cucumber. Slice the celery diagonally. Toss the salad ingredients in a bowl with the sage and chive flowers.*

2 *Mix the olive oil with the lemon juice and seasoning and spoon over the salad. Toss lightly before serving.*

LATE SUMMER SALAD WITH NASTURTIUMS

- SERVES 4–6
- INGREDIENTS
  about 16 young nasturtium
    leaves
  mixed salad leaves
  2–3 boiled beetroot (beets)
  about 16 whole nasturtium
    flowers, stems removed
  about 4–6 nasturtium flower
    buds

For the dressing
4 crushed nasturtium seeds
60ml/4 tbsp walnut or
  olive oil
10ml/2 tsp white wine or
  balsamic vinegar
coarse salt and ground
  black pepper

1 *Create an outer wall of young nasturtium leaves around the edge of a deep salad bowl. Add an inner wall of mixed salad leaves.*

2 *Slice the beetroot very thinly and place in layers between the two types of salad leaves.*

3 *Decorate with nasturtium flowers and buds, leaving a whole flower for the centre.*

4 *Mix together the dressing ingredients and pour over the salad before serving.*

Left and right: *Late Summer Salad with Nasturtiums.*

spring enchantment

wild delights daisies galore

regal rosemary **sweet cicely**

chive and parsley partners

magnificent marigolds

blue blooms pleasing pinks

aromatic thyme **citrus scents**

soothing lavender

elderflower treats

Plant
Schemes

So many edible flowers are a joy to grow as well as to eat. Here are a number of planting ideas which provide detailed information on how to make stunning arrangements in the garden, with wonderful recipes to make the most of the bountiful crops of flowers. Both the planting and culinary ideas are explained step by step, guaranteeing success for gardeners and cooks alike.

Right: Scented geranium leaves smell heavenly in the garden and can be used to great effect in the kitchen, too.

Early Spring
Enchantment

Right: Violets are one of the first spring flowers to bloom and will soon spread to form a dense carpet.

Sweet violets are a semi-evergreen perennial from southern and western Europe, growing 8–10cm/3–4in high. They will naturalize easily in partial shade. They have small, very fragrant blue or white flowers which appear in late winter to early spring. They sometimes flower again in the autumn. They form tufts of thick rhizomes and spread by means of runners. They can also be propagated by seed. Parma violets are also very scented, with slightly larger blue, pink, purple or white flowers. In recent years these have become more easy to obtain, and are now readily available from garden centres or, in the United States, from edible flower suppliers. They are certainly worth seeking out for their colour, scent and flavour.

Primroses are also perennial and are always welcome in the garden, for both their delicate scent and colouring. They are native throughout Europe and thrive well in partial shade with some moisture. In dry seasons they might lose their leaves in late summer, but will return in the autumn. They can be divided easily in spring and autumn.

Left: Primroses self-seed easily and will soon find a shady spot beneath a hedge where they can make themselves at home.

in the garden

BLUE AND WHITE VIOLETS WITH PRIMROSES AND GOLDEN FEVERFEW

Violets and primroses make natural bedfellows in an early spring pot. Golden feverfew adds brightness of leaf and together they make a delightful container which is full of scent and sweet flavours.

- INGREDIENTS
  1 blue violet plant *Viola odorata*
  2 white violet plants *Viola odorata*
  1 primrose plant *Primula vulgaris*
  2 golden feverfew plants *Tanacetum parthenium* 'Aurea'

- DRAINAGE Old crocks (china), grit (gravel) or small pieces of polystyrene (plastic foam)
- COMPOST (SOIL MIX) Use fresh compost in containers. Choose either a soil-based compost or a proprietary potting compost (planting mix)
- CONTAINER A medium-sized pot, 36cm/14in wide and 17.5cm/7in deep, was used

here. However, this combination would suit different containers, including larger pots, wooden half barrels and wicker baskets
- SITE Sun or shade
- WHEN TO PLANT Late winter
- AT ITS BEST Early to mid-spring

1 *Prepare the pot for planting by covering the base with 2.5cm/1in of drainage material.*

2 *Add compost to a depth of about 5cm/2in.*

3 *Arrange the plants around the edge of the pot, with the blue violet in the centre.*

4 *Fill in any gaps with compost, bringing the compost level to within 2.5cm/1in of the top of the container. Water well. Firm in the plants and add more compost if necessary.*

AFTERCARE

It is important to keep the compost moist at all times. Remember to remove flowers as they fade in order to encourage further production. Pick only the freshest ones for use in the kitchen. After flowering has finished, the plants may be transferred to a shady place in the garden or moved on to a larger pot for another show next season.

Sweet violets have been a great favourite in the kitchen for hundreds of years. Violet wine was a popular drink among the Persians and Romans, while in Tudor days in England, syrups, conserves and violet candy drops were commonly used. Recipes from the 17th century suggest that violet-flavoured honey was enjoyed in France, while in England young violet leaves were first fried and then eaten with sugar flavoured with orange and lemon. Primroses (sometimes referred to as primmy roses) have also been used for generations to candy and crystallize and to make delicious wine. Although feverfew leaves are eaten by migraine sufferers, they are extremely bitter and not to be recommended for general cooking purposes. The following idea adapts the old tradition of using primroses and violets as strewing flowers in salads.

Above: Primroses and violets make a pretty addition to any spring salad. They are also lovely as a garnish on pâté or as a simple decoration on a cake.

in the kitchen ## EARLY SPRING SALAD

Violets and primrose flowers will add flavour and colour to any spring salad. Simply mix your favourite ingredients and arrange the flowers on top. Here, blue violets and yellow primroses look very inviting against pale avocado and creamy goat's cheese. Pick only the freshest blooms (ideally on a dry morning), place the stems in water and use the same day.

- SERVES **4**
- INGREDIENTS
  2 spring onions (scallions)
  2 ripe avocados
  30ml/2 tbsp lemon juice
  150g/5oz mild goat's cheese
  small handful each of
    primroses and violets

For the dressing
90ml/6 tbsp light olive oil
30ml/2 tbsp white wine
  vinegar (see opposite for
  violet vinegar alternative)
5ml/1 tsp dry mustard
5ml/1 tsp caster (superfine)
  sugar
salt and ground black pepper

1 To make the dressing, use a fork to mix together all the ingredients in a bowl. Chill in the refrigerator until required.

2 △ Trim the spring onions. Cut lengthways into thin shreds, then across into 5cm/2in lengths. Put in a bowl of cold water so that the shreds curl. Leave in a cool place for an hour.

3 △ Halve and stone (pit) the avocados and peel away the skins. Slice very finely and toss in a bowl with lemon juice to prevent discoloration. Cut the cheese into small pieces. Remove all the green parts from the flowers.

4 To serve, scatter the avocado and cheese on to serving plates and add the drained spring onions. Finish with the primrose and violet flowers and spoon over the dressing.

VIOLET VINEGAR

As a delicious alternative to basic vinaigrette, add violet vinegar in place of white wine vinegar. Violet vinegar is made by placing petals from scented blue violets in white wine vinegar for about four weeks. Use a screw-top jar and fill to the top with violets and vinegar. Screw the top securely and then place on a sunny windowsill. The sun helps release all the oils from the flowers. Shake occasionally and, when the liquid has turned blue, strain and use as required. Mix up a vinaigrette to serve with the Early Spring Salad, or try it with seafood salads or grilled vegetables. Parma violets also make an excellent vinaigrette; either purple or pink, they are now easily available in spring. Fortunately, violets flower over a period of several weeks so it is possible to make more than one batch.

Rustic Delights

Cowslips were once one of the most popular of all spring culinary flowers and, although numbers of wild plants have plummeted in our own lifetimes, they are still seen in areas with alkaline soil. They are now readily available either as seed or as growing plants and they can be grown in borders, grassland or containers. The wild flower seeds tend to produce much smaller plants than cultivated cowslips, which are the ones more often sold as plants in garden centres. Whether you choose cultivated cowslips or the wild variety to grow yourself, once established they will soon produce entire colonies. Their uses in the kitchen are plentiful.

Above: Cowslips self-seed very easily, especially in limestone areas among grass or in borders.

in the garden ## RUSTIC BASKET OF COWSLIPS UNDERPLANTED WITH VIOLAS AND VARIEGATED MINT

The dainty heads of yellow cowslips look charming growing alongside pretty blue violas and the delicate creamy markings of variegated mint. They make a versatile combination. The cowslip and viola flowers and mint leaves (and later the mint flowers) can be used to add colour and variety to both green and fruit salads. In addition, both the cowslip and viola flowers, as well as the young mint leaves, can be successfully crystallized and used in a variety of mouthwatering ways on fruit fools, mousses, roulades, trifles and cakes.

- INGREDIENTS
  4 cowslip plants *Primula veris*
  4 viola plants *Viola* 'Penny'
  1 large variegated applemint plant *Mentha suaveolens* 'Variegata'

- DRAINAGE Old crocks (china), grit (gravel) or pieces of polystyrene (plastic foam)
- LINER Black plastic lining from the bottom of a refuse sack (garbage bag), cut generously to fit the depth of the basket. Any excess can be rolled over at the top when the planting is complete
- COMPOST (SOIL MIX) Use fresh compost in containers. Choose either a soil-based compost or a proprietary potting compost (planting mix)
- CONTAINER A medium-sized wicker basket 45cm/18in long 30cm/12in wide and

15cm/6in deep was used here. It has been given three coats of "yacht" varnish both inside and outside to preserve it for outdoor use. This combination would also suit many medium-sized containers, including window boxes and wall pots
- SITE Sun or partial shade. Raise on a table or wall so that you can really enjoy it
- WHEN TO PLANT Early spring
- AT ITS BEST Mid- to late spring

1 △ *Line the basket with the cut-down black plastic refuse sack and cut four slits in the base to allow excess water to drain through.*

2 △ *Cover the base of the container with 2.5cm/1in drainage material and add compost to a depth of about 5cm/2in.*

3 △ *Plant two cowslips in the corners on one side of the basket and position the third under the opposite handle. Then arrange three violas in opposite positions.*

4 △ *Plant the mint in the centre with another cowslip and viola on either side. Fill in any gaps with compost, bringing the compost to within 2.5cm/1in of the top of the container. Water well. Firm in the plants and add more compost if necessary. Tuck in any excess plastic beneath the rim of the basket.*

GARDENER'S TIP
Once planted, lift the basket from underneath. The handle will not be strong enough to support the weight of the filled basket.

AFTERCARE
Keep the compost moist at all times. Remember to remove flowers as they fade in order to encourage further production. Pick only the freshest ones for use in the kitchen. After the cowslips and violas have finished flowering, move the cowslips and mint to a sunny part of the garden or to a larger pot for another show next season. Clean and re-varnish the basket before replanting. The mint will grow into a large plant in the garden and will look lovely in a herb bed or near some roses. It will flower in late summer. The cowslips will grow on well in borders or grassy areas of the garden but they like moisture.

in the kitchen

Right: *Pick only the freshest blooms, ideally on a dry morning. Place the stems in water and use the same day.*

The warmer days of spring herald the cowslip with its dainty array of sweet-smelling flowers. These "pips", as they were once commonly known, were gathered in huge quantities to be made into cowslip wine, with yeast, sugar and oranges, or into cowslip mead, using honey and lemon. Smaller quantities were collected to make cowslip cream and cowslip pudding. They were even preserved with vinegar and sugar as cowslip pickle.

CRYSTALLIZED COWSLIPS AND VIOLAS

Crystallized violas and cowslips may be used as decorations on cakes, cookies, roulades, mousses, and other desserts. They look lovely on layer cakes or whipped cream. If you use the gum arabic method then you can preserve the flowers for summer use as well.

METHOD 1
- INGREDIENTS

  1 egg white
  30ml/2 tbsp caster
  (superfine) sugar
  a handful of cowslip
  flowers, all stalks and
  green parts removed
  a handful of viola
  flowers, all stalks and
  green parts removed
  sprigs of mint

1 *Remove the white heels of petals before crystallizing. Lightly beat the egg white and, using a small brush, coat each petal, front and back, with the egg white.*

2 *Lightly sprinkle caster sugar over the petals, front and back. It will cling to the moist surface.*

3 *Taking care to retain the shape as much as possible, Place the flowers on parchment paper, on a plate or wire rack and keep in a warm place until crisp and dry. Store them in an airtight tin or jar. They can be kept for up to 2 days.*

METHOD 2
- INGREDIENTS

  as above but substitute
  gum arabic for egg white
  25ml/1fl oz/1½ tbsp
  water or colourless spirit
  (alcohol)

USING GUM ARABIC (available from the chemist)

1 *Dissolve 5 ml/1 tsp of gum arabic in 1fl oz/25 ml/1½ tbsp of water or a colourless spirit such as vodka or gin.*

2 *Paint each petal with the mixture and sprinkle with caster sugar.*

3 *Dry on a rack in a warm place until crisp. Flowers crystallized in this way keep for several months.*

in the kitchen   ## COWSLIP SYLLABUB

Crystallized cowslips and violas make a delightful addition to many sweet dishes. Here they are used together to add artistry to a simple syllabub. Pretty variegated mint adds the final touch.

- SERVES 4–6
- INGREDIENTS

200ml/7fl oz medium white
    wine
60ml/4 tbsp caster
    (superfine) sugar
finely grated rind and juice of
    1 orange
300ml/½ pint/1¼ cups fresh
    double (heavy) cream

1 *Place the wine, sugar, orange rind and juice in a bowl and leave to stand for 2 hours or more.*

2 *Add the mixture to the cream a little at a time, whisking all the time until the mixture stands in soft peaks.*

3 *Spoon a little syllabub into the base of four to six wine glasses. Add a few crystallized viola petals and a few cowslips, facing outwards so that they show through the glass. Add more syllabub in the middle of each glass. Create a peak in the centre of each glass.*

4 *Chill before serving. Decorate with a scattering of crystallized cowslips and violas and add a few mint leaves to each glass.*

COOK'S TIP
Make the crystallized flowers the day before the syllabub so that they have the chance to dry.

Left: Using crystallized violas to decorate a cake makes it pretty enough for a special occasion. Cover the cake in an orange or lemon flavoured icing first – the citrus tang perfectly complements the delicate scent of the flowers.

Daisies Galore

aisies flower prolifically in spring and early summer and provide a wonderful array of colour in the garden among other spring-flowering plants, such as violas and primroses. They are extremely versatile and can be grown in any container, large or small. They would make a delightful spring hanging basket partnered with cowslips and rosemary. In this pot, three different-coloured daisies and sweet woodruff make a sumptuous display around a gold-tipped marjoram. By late spring the sweet woodruff will be a mass of white flowers. When sweet woodruff is dried, its leaves smell of new-mown hay. In the past, the leaves were often kept in little sachets to scent pillows and clothes. Both woodruff flowers and leaves can be used to flavour wine, and this tradition still lives on in Germany.

Above: The gold-tipped marjoram peeps out among the daisies. Double daisies are commonly available in pink, red and white. Use all one colour or mix them together to provide a sumptuous tapestry effect.

in the garden ## DAISIES, SWEET WOODRUFF AND MARJORAM POT

Daisies and marjoram are easy to buy in early spring, but if the sweet woodruff proves difficult to find, you could substitute violas or parsley. Daisies will combine beautifully with both. Alternatively, just use the daisies on their own – nothing could be simpler.

- **INGREDIENTS**
  1 pink daisy plant *Bellis perennis* 'Tasso Rose'
  1 red daisy plant *Bellis perennis* 'Tasso Red'
  1 white daisy plant *Bellis perennis* 'Tasso White'
  3 sweet woodruff plants *Galium odoratum*
  1 gold-tipped marjoram plant *Origanum vulgare* 'Gold Tip'

- **DRAINAGE** Old crocks (china), grit (gravel) or pieces of polystyrene (plastic foam)
- **COMPOST (SOIL MIX)** Use fresh compost. Choose either a soil-based compost or a proprietary potting compost (planting mix)
- **CONTAINER** A medium-sized pot, 30cm/12in wide and 15cm/6in deep, was used here. However, the combination would suit many different containers, including larger pots, wall pots and hanging baskets

- **SITE** Sun or shade
- **WHEN TO PLANT** Early spring
- **AT ITS BEST** Mid- to late spring (although the marjoram will flower later in summer)

1 △ *Prepare the pot for planting by covering the base with 2.5cm/1in of drainage material.*

2 △ *Add compost to a depth of about 5cm/2in. Space the three sweet woodruff around the edge of the pot.*

3 △ *Plant the daisies in the gaps between the sweet woodruff to create a pleasing arrangement.*

4 △ *Plant the marjoram in the centre. Fill in any gaps with compost bringing the compost to within 2.5cm/1in of the top of the container. Water well. Firm in the plants and add more compost if necessary.*

AFTERCARE

It is important to keep the compost moist at all times. Remember to remove flowers as they fade in order to encourage further production. Pick only the freshest ones for use in the kitchen. Discard the daisies when they have finished flowering and transfer the sweet woodruff to a shady spot in the garden where it will form a carpet beneath shrubs or beside the path. The marjoram can be left in the pot or moved to a sunny position in the garden. Either way, it will flower beautifully and attract lots of butterflies.

Right: *The daisy pot nestles among a sea of sweet cicely.*

in the kitchen

In the past, young daisy leaves were used in salads and, in Italy and Spain, even the roots were eaten. Here, the flowers are the highlight, with every flower providing a multitude of quills to scatter over all kinds of fruity mousses, ice creams, cakes and savoury dishes. The flowers are so generous in their bounty that just one plant will provide enough material for a feast.

Above: Pink, red or white daisy petals can be scattered in patterns or at random on cakes or desserts. Marjoram leaves can be combined with daisy petals to garnish a savoury pâté dish or green salad.

in the kitchen

BLACKCURRANT MOUSSE WITH DAISIES

Here, daisy petals add a simple, carefree topping to this blackcurrant dessert. They look pretty with rhubarb or gooseberry, too. In fact, they are extremely versatile.

• SERVES 4–6 PEOPLE
• INGREDIENTS
- 800g/1lb 12oz fresh or frozen blackcurrants
- 150g/5oz caster (superfine) sugar
- 450ml/¾ pint/scant 2 cups natural (plain) yogurt

• TO DECORATE
  Pink and red daisies
  Sprigs of blackcurrants

1 *Strip the blackcurrants off the stalks and put in a pan with 90ml/6 tbsp water and the sugar. Cover tightly and simmer gently for about 10 minutes until the fruit is pulpy. Blend in a food processor, then press through a sieve (strainer) and leave to cool.*

2 *Stir the yogurt into the purée until evenly combined, then spoon the mixture into serving glasses and chill until ready to serve.*

3 *Add the blackcurrants to the top of each, then gently pull the quills from the daisies and scatter over the top.*

COOK'S TIP
For a richer flavour, fold the same quantity of lightly whipped cream into the blackcurrant purée instead of the natural yogurt.

in the kitchen **DAISY CAKES**

What could be prettier for afternoon tea or a children's party than these scrumptious little cakes decorated with daisy petals? The daisy centre is made from coloured icing (frosting).

- MAKES 15–20
- INGREDIENTS

  115g/4oz butter or
  margarine, softened

  115g/4oz caster (superfine)
  sugar

  2 medium eggs

  115g/4oz self-raising (self-
  rising) flour

  2.5ml/½ tsp baking powder

  10ml/2 tsp lemon juice

- TO DECORATE

  115g/4oz icing
  (confectioners') sugar

  1 tbsp water

  dash of yellow food colouring

  2–3 daisies

1 *Preheat the oven to 180ºC/350ºF/Gas 4. Line sections of a tartlet tin (cupcake pan) with paper cake cases. Put the butter or margarine in a bowl with the sugar and eggs. Sift the flour and baking powder into the bowl. Add the lemon juice and beat until pale and creamy.*

2 *Spoon the mixture into the cases and bake for about 15 minutes until risen and golden. Transfer to a wire rack and leave to cool.*

3 *Beat the icing sugar with a little water until the glaze thinly coats the back of the spoon. Add a dash of yellow food colouring to match the centre of real daisy flowers.*

4 △ *Spoon a little icing on to each cake. Gently pull the quills from a daisy and use to decorate. Repeat with the remainder of the cakes.*

Regal Rosemary

Right: *In times past, rosemary flowers were used for tonics and drinks of all kinds.*

Rosemary is an evergreen herb full of scent and flavour. It complements many other beautiful plants, both in spring when it is in full flower itself and also in summer, when its distinctive shape and foliage set it in pleasing contrast with other flowering plants such as sage and roses. In cooler climates, it prefers the shelter of a wall to an exposed site. It will grow well in containers, large or small.

Rosemary usually has pale blue flowers, but there is also a much darker blue form called 'Benenden Blue' and a pink called 'Majorca Pink'. Whatever the colour, the flowers can all be used for the same purpose.

in the garden

TAPESTRY WITH ROSEMARY

This spring hanging basket can be created using many different combinations of edible flowers and herbs, depending on individual preferences for colour and flavour. The violas are available in a range of blue, purple, yellow, cream, white and bicolours, while the double daisies are available in white, pink or red. Mixed with a range of golden herb foliage such as golden marjoram, golden lemon balm and golden feverfew, the effect is like a beautiful tapestry. Planting need not be complicated – just remember to position the mints and lemon balm near the bottom of the basket and the rosemary at the top. The sides are up to you.

- **INGREDIENTS**
- 1 golden lemon balm plant *Melissa officinalis* 'Aurea'
- 1 variegated applemint plant *Mentha suaveolens* 'Variegata'
- 1 eau-de-cologne mint plant *Mentha x piperata f. citrata*
- 2 viola plants *Viola* 'Penny'
- 3 golden feverfew plants *Tanacetum parthenium*
- 1 marjoram plant *Oregano vulgare*
- 2 red daisy plants *Bellis perennis* 'Tasso Red'
- 5 parsley plants *Petroselinum crispum*
- 1 rosemary plant *Rosmarinus officinalis*
- 2 cowslip plants *Primula veris*
- 1 pink daisy plant *Bellis perennis* 'Tasso Rose'

- **MOSS**
- **LINER** Circle of plastic sheeting (can be cut from the compost bag), the size of a salad plate
- **COMPOST (SOIL MIX)** Use fresh compost. Choose either a soil-based compost or a proprietary potting compost (planting mix)
- **CONTAINER** 35cm/14in-diameter wire hanging basket
- **SITE** Sun or partial shade
- **WHEN TO PLANT** Early spring
- **AT ITS BEST** Mid- to late spring

Left: *Rosemary has exquisite pale blue flowers which are produced all the way along the stems, so that a rosemary bush in full flower is a haze of blue.*

GARDENER'S TIP

Many daisies, violas and parsleys can be bought very reasonably as small plants growing in strips or polystyrene (plastic foam) cells. These work out much cheaper than individual pots of plants. Another advantage is that their roots are smaller and therefore easier to push through the sides of the basket. Don't be afraid to use herbs already growing in the garden. Golden feverfew may have self-seeded in abundance and mints and marjorams will divide easily at this time of year.

1 △ *Line the base of the basket with a generous layer of moss. Cover with the circle of plastic sheeting and a thin layer of compost. Plant the bottom layer of herbs with the variegated lemon balm in the centre and the two mints to each side, leaving a gap of about 8–10cm/3–4in between the lemon balm and the mint. This method assumes that the basket will be hung against a wall and so the back has fewer plants. Make sure all the roots have good contact with the compost.*

2 △ *Add a collar of moss around each plant and bring the wall of moss about one-third of the way up the sides of the basket. Add compost to a depth of about 5cm/2in. Plant the two violas in the gaps between the lemon balm and mints. Plant two golden feverfew at the same level but further round the sides. Secure each plant with more moss, bringing the level to about two-thirds of the way up the sides of the basket.*

3 △ *Plant an upper ring with the marjoram, feverfew and a daisy around the front, and two parsley plants either side. Bring the wall of moss to about 2.5cm/1in above the rim of the basket, which allows for the moss to settle as the top planting is completed and the basket is watered.*

4 △ *Plant the rosemary towards the centre back of the basket, with the cowslips on either side and the daisies in front. Plant the three parsley plants around the edge of the basket. Fill in any gaps with compost. Water well and firm in the plants. Add more compost and moss if necessary.*

AFTERCARE

It is important to keep the compost (soil mix) moist at all times. Remember to remove flowers as they fade in order to encourage further production. Pick only the freshest ones for use in the kitchen including the daisies, cowslips and violas and later the marjoram. Feverfew is sometimes eaten by migraine sufferers but it tastes very bitter. The rosemary might not flower the first year but it will thereafter. Feed with a liquid plant food monthly throughout the summer. In the autumn, empty the basket, transferring the rosemary to a pot where it can continue to grow next year. Separate the other herbs and edible flowers, discard the daisies and violas but pot the rest on individually or transfer to the garden.

Right: *The sides of the basket soon create a sumptuous tapestry.*

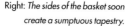

in the kitchen

osemary flowers taste very much like the leaf but with a residual sweetness from the base of the flower, which makes them suitable for use in both sweet and savoury dishes. A favourite use of the plant in the 16th century was to make rosemary water from the leaves and flowers combined. Another delight of the time involved candied rosemary flowers. There are recipes for rosemary "snow" made with egg whites and cream, rosemary tea using just the leaves, and rosemary wine in which white wine is flavoured with rosemary.

Right: Rosemary flowers can be eaten fresh with many savoury foods.

in the kitchen

ROSEMARY BISCUITS (CRACKERS)

Here the flowers are used to flavour and garnish the top of savoury rosemary biscuits (crackers), which are delicious either on their own or with a mild-flavoured cheese.

- MAKES ABOUT 25
- INGREDIENTS
  225g/8oz plain (all-purpose) flour
  2.5ml/½ tsp baking powder
  good pinch of salt
  2.5ml/½ tsp curry powder

  75g/3oz butter
  30ml/2 tbsp finely chopped young rosemary leaves
  1 egg yolk
  milk, to glaze
  - TO DECORATE
    30ml/2 tbsp cream cheese
    rosemary flowers

1 *Put the flour, baking powder, salt and curry powder in a food processor. Add the butter, cut into small pieces, and blend until the mixture resembles fine breadcrumbs. Add the rosemary, egg yolk and 30–45ml/2–3 tbsp cold water and mix to a firm dough. (Alternatively rub the butter into the flour mixture in a bowl, then add the remaining ingredients and combine.) Chill in the refrigerator for 30 minutes.*

2 *Preheat the oven to 180ºC/ 350ºF/Gas 4. Thinly roll the dough on a lightly floured surface and cut out the biscuits (crackers) using a 5cm/2in plain or fluted cutter.*

3 *Transfer to a large baking sheet and prick with a fork. Brush with milk to glaze and bake for about 10 minutes until pale golden. Transfer to a wire rack and leave to cool.*

4 △ *Spread a little cream cheese on to each biscuit and secure a few rosemary flowers on top, using tweezers to position the flowers, if easier.*

Sweet Cicely

Sweet cicely is native to southern Europe but is now widespread throughout Europe and western Asia. It loves a moist, shady spot where it will colonize quickly. It is an attractive herbaceous perennial with a long tap root and a wealth of large, fern-like leaves which emerge in early spring. By late spring the tall stalks bear flat umbrels of tiny white flowers. All top growth dies back by late autumn and should be removed.

Left: Sweet cicely flowers are produced over a period of several weeks in late spring and early summer.

in the garden

Sweet cicely is a great asset to the edible flower garden, producing quantities of sweet aniseed-flavoured flowers and leaves in late spring and early summer. By mid- to late summer, the seeds ripen to black and can be crushed to impart their characteristic aniseed flavour. This is a plant with many culinary uses. It is easy to grow and a pleasure to use. The only drawback is its ability to self-seed. You need to be very strict and take off all unwanted ripe seeds or be very sure to remove all unwanted seedlings early in the summer. Otherwise, once established they are difficult to remove on account of their very deep tap root.

Left: When fully ripe, the seeds of the sweet cicely plant turn black. Unless the seeds are required for winter keeping, deadhead the plants before they reach this stage to prevent a mass of seedlings in the spring.

Above: Sweet cicely can be wrongly mistaken for cow parsley, which it resembles in both leaf and flower. However, there are two distinct differences. First, all parts of sweet cicely impart a sweet aniseed flavour when crushed. Second, sweet cicely leaves often bear a white blotch.

GARDENER'S TIP

Semi-ripe seeds taste of sweet aniseed and are delicious to nibble on while pottering about the garden. They should be picked when newly formed, otherwise they soon form a tough outer coating which makes them stringy. Toss them in salads or add to roast (bell) peppers to impart extra flavour.

in the kitchen

Right: *Sweet cicely flowers
taste of aniseed and have
many uses in the kitchen.*

On account of its high sugar content, sweet cicely has long been used as a sugar substitute in the cooking of tart fruit such as gooseberries, rhubarb and damsons. When cooking with sweet cicely, only use about half the normal amount of sugar. Use the flowers, leaves and crushed seeds in drinks, fruit salads, soups and fish sauces. Even the tap root can be boiled and eaten.

in the kitchen ## ROASTED PEPPERS WITH SWEET CICELY

• SERVES 4

• INGREDIENTS

4 red (bell) peppers, halved
   and deseeded
8 small or 4 medium tomatoes
15ml/1 tbsp semi-ripe sweet
   cicely seeds
15ml/1 tbsp fennel seeds
15ml/1 tbsp capers
8 sweet cicely flowers, newly
   opened, stems removed
60ml/4 tbsp olive oil

This is a dish full of flavour with a beautiful, intense colour to match. The red peppers are cooked with tomatoes and scattered with semi-ripe sweet cicely seeds, fennel seeds and capers, with sweet cicely flowers added on top. The whole dish is then roasted with lashings of olive oil. The sweet aniseed flavours combine beautifully with the capers and the succulent taste of the tomatoes and peppers. Sweet cicely leaves make an excellent garnish and they taste just like the flowers. This dish can be served as a appetizer or light lunch.

• GARNISH

   a few small sweet cicely leaves
   8 more flowers, newly
      opened, stems removed

1 ◁ *Place the red pepper halves in a large ovenproof dish. To skin the tomatoes, cut a cross at the base, then pour over boiling water and leave to stand for five minutes. Cut them in half if they are of medium size. Fill each halved red pepper cavity with a whole small tomato, or half a medium tomato.*

2 ◁ *Cover with a scattering of semi-ripe sweet cicely seeds, fennel seeds and capers and about half the sweet cicely flowers. Drizzle the olive oil all over. Bake in the top of the oven for 1 hour. Remove from the oven and add the rest of the flowers. Serve garnished with fresh sweet cicely leaves and flowers, and lots of crusty bread to soak up the juices.*

Chive and
Parsley Partners

Right: *Every chive flower-head is made up of 30 or 40 florets. Each one has a mild oniony flavour with lots of crunch.*

Below: *Chives grow from small bulbs which soon multiply to produce large clumps. All the growth dies down during the winter months.*

Chives are one of our best-known culinary herbs, producing long, grass-like stems which taste of mild onion from spring right through the summer. They can be planted in the garden, where they will grow into large clumps and flower in early summer, or sown from seed in early spring, which will produce flowers in mid-summer. The lilac-pink flowers are extremely pretty, full of flavour and they have a crunchy bite which makes them an asset to many culinary dishes. This pot contains a clump of chives transplanted from the garden and surrounded with young parsley seedlings. Chives and parsley make a marvellous partnership – both to the eye and to the tastebuds.

Chives are an easy garden plant to grow from seed and will keep growing for many years, although it is best to divide them every three years or so. They also grow well in pots, if kept moist.

in the garden   CHIVE AND PARSLEY POT

Parsley and chives are partners in so many cooking recipes that it seems highly appropriate to grow them together. Chives are by no means the neatest of plants, but in this arrangement, they can grow to their hearts' content, surrounded by a collar of fresh green parsley which helps to keep their sprawling leaves in check.

- INGREDIENTS
  1 large clump of chives *Allium schoenoprasum*
  3 pots of parsley seedlings (or single plants) *Petroselinum crispum*
  (If you are using young chive plants, choose two pots of chives and two of parsley, planted opposite each other)

- DRAINAGE Old crocks (china), grit (gravel) or small pieces of polystyrene (plastic foam)
- COMPOST (SOIL MIX) Use fresh compost in containers. Choose either a soil-based compost or a proprietary potting compost (planting mix)
- CONTAINER A medium-sized pot, 30cm/12in wide and 17.5cm/7in deep, was used here. However, this combination is also suitable for window-boxes and wall pots
- SITE Sun or partial shade
- WHEN TO PLANT Late spring
- AT ITS BEST Early to mid-summer

1 *Prepare the pot for planting by covering the base with 2.5cm/1in of drainage material and add about 5cm/2in of compost.*

2 *Plant the clump of chives in the centre of the pot. Gently remove the parsley seedlings from their pots and plant around the chives.*

3 *Fill in any gaps in the arrangement with compost, bringing the compost to within 2.5cm/1in of the top of the container. Water well. Firm in the plants and add more compost if necessary.*

AFTERCARE

It is very important to keep the compost moist at all times, especially during the growing period. The leaves can be cut back at least once before you allow the plant to flower. Remember to remove flowers as they fade in order to encourage further production. Pick only the freshest ones for use in the kitchen. The chives will send up flowers for many weeks, even after the main flush is over. Use the parsley regularly to encourage fresh growth. It will self-seed if allowed.

in the kitchen

Above: *Mix chive and sage flowers for a pretty and tasty butter to be offered with baked potatoes (see page 23).*

Make sure you position this pot near the kitchen because the parsley and chives can be used together in many dishes. The leaves of both plants and the chive flowers can be combined to add great flavour to salads, white sauces for fish and baked ham, simple pasta dishes and fillings for rolls, bagels and baguettes. Prepare some chive-flower butter for serving with potatoes or carrots, or try a butter blended with a mix of sage and chive flowers. Another successful combination is to mix some chive flowers with marigold petals and serve them on top of baked potatoes. It tastes wonderful and makes a very colourful decoration.

The fragrant, starry white flowers of *Allium tuberosum*, better known as garlic chives, can be used in the same way, although the flavour is more of garlic than onion.

in the kitchen

SCRAMBLED EGGS WITH CHIVE FLOWERS

- SERVES 2
- INGREDIENTS
  30ml/2 tbsp chive flowers
  (pick only the freshest
  flower-heads)
  30ml/2 tbsp chopped chive
  leaves (pick young leaves)
  15ml/1 tbsp chopped
  parsley (pick the freshest
  leaves)
  4 eggs
  salt and ground black pepper
  60ml/4 tbsp milk or cream
  50g/2oz butter

- TO SERVE
  4 slices of buttered toast

COOK'S TIP
Chive-flavoured scrambled egg can be used as a sandwich filling or topping for bagels.

Scrambled eggs on toast is one of the simplest and quickest meals, taking only a matter of minutes to prepare and cook. By adding finely chopped parsley and chive leaves and a handful of lilac-pink chive flowers, it is transformed into something much more tasty and certainly far more imaginative.

1 △ *Cut the chive flower-heads from the main stem, then snip off each floret, removing as much of the little stems as possible. You will probably have between 30 and 40 individual florets from each flower-head.*

2 *Chop the chive leaves and parsley very finely and mix with the chive flowers.*

3 *Beat or whisk the eggs and seasoning together with the milk.*

4 △ *Melt the butter in a heavy pan. Pour in the egg mixture and cook over a low heat. Stir continuously for a minute or two until the mixture is just beginning to thicken, then add the chive leaves and flowers and the parsley.*

5 *Serve the scrambled eggs with buttered toast and add a scattering of extra flowers as a garnish.*

Magnificent Marigolds

Above: With such brilliant colouring, no wonder one of the old names for pot marigolds was "golds".

Pot marigolds are a hardy annual native to southern Europe and north Africa, which grow about 30cm/ 12in high and across. They are generous in flower, producing a feast of petals with every single flower-head. With their vibrant orange colouring, they make a lovely display either in the garden, where they will happily self-seed year after year, or in a pot. Either way they are easy to grow. Those that are self-sown will start to flower very early in the year, whereas marigold seed sown in the spring will not produce flowers until mid-summer. However, if the plants are dead-headed, they will continue to blossom until the very end of the year in a mild season. It is for this reason that marigolds earned their Latin name *Calendula* because they were reputed to flower on the first day of every month in the year.

Nowadays many cultivars are available, including 'Fiesta Gitana', with pastel orange and yellow flowers, as well as bicolours and 'Orange Queen' and 'Lemon Queen' with their double orange and yellow flowers respectively.

in the garden MARIGOLD AND PARSLEY POT

This is a delightfully simple scheme which produces masses of bright orange pot marigold flowers seen against a mound of frilly green parsley. The attractive sage green pot sets the combination off beautifully.

- INGREDIENTS
  4 pot marigold plants
  Calendula officinalis
  1 parsley plant *Petroselinum crispum*

  WARNING
  Pot marigolds, *Calendula officinalis*, are the culinary marigolds described here, **not** the so-called African marigolds, which are botanically named *Tagetes*.

- DRAINAGE Old crocks (china), grit (gravel) or pieces of polystyrene (plastic foam)
- COMPOST (SOIL MIX) Use fresh compost in containers. Choose either a soil-based compost or a proprietary potting compost (planting mix). Add water-retaining crystals before planting
- CONTAINER This is a large

pot, 38cm/15in diameter and 25cm/10in deep. A wooden half barrel would also be suitable
- SITE Sun or partial shade
- WHEN TO PLANT Early to mid-spring
- AT ITS BEST Mid-summer to autumn

1 △ *Prepare the container for planting by covering the base with 5cm/2in drainage material. Add compost to a depth of about 5cm/2in. Plant the four marigolds around the edge of the container.*

2 △ *Plant the parsley in the centre of the pot. Fill in any gaps with compost, bringing the compost to within 2.5cm/1in of the top of the container. Water well. Firm in the plants and add more compost if necessary.*

AFTERCARE

Keep the compost moist at all times. Pick only the freshest blooms for use in the kitchen. Cut off all flower-heads as soon as they are past their best in order to encourage further production. This is very important in order to lengthen the flowering season. Use the parsley as needed. Discard the contents of the pot at the end of the autumn but you can save some of the marigold seeds for next year's crop.

in the kitchen

Above: *Pot marigold petals make a simple but colourful addition to salads and many other dishes.*

Above: *To prepare for cooking, remove each petal from the flower head. It is surprising how the flowers can look completely orange and yet the individual petals are only orange at the tip. Yellow pot marigold heads are just as suitable as orange ones.*

Pot marigolds were a great favourite in Persian and Greek cooking and later all around the Mediterranean, where they were often dried in great quantities and used in winter stews and soups. In England, many people preferred them pickled in salt and water, rather than dried. They were also common in salads, conserves and syrups. There were recipes for marigold pudding, with lots of cream, breadcrumbs and suet. Marigold wine was another treat, in which the flowers were used for both colour and flavour.

Today, marigold petals are useful in all sorts of ways. They have a light, tangy flavour and are packed with rich colour. As well as in salads, try them with spirals of pasta, scatter them with chopped parsley on top of baked potatoes, add them to a lamb casserole or to a white sauce to accompany fish. Make marigold butter, mix them in omelettes, add them to hard-boiled eggs, or use them in rice dishes where they will greatly enhance the colour. Marigold flowers are so versatile, it is no wonder they were once so popular.

in the kitchen

MARIGOLD SALAD WITH CURRIED EGGS

- SERVES 4
- INGREDIENTS

4 medium eggs

5ml/1 tsp mild curry powder or paste

75ml/5 tbsp mayonnaise

60ml/4 tbsp single (light) cream

15ml/1 tbsp chopped parsley

1 bag of mixed salad leaves with light and dark red lettuce

1 pot marigold head, using the petals only

This dressing has a mild, creamy curry flavour and looks lovely poured over semi-soft boiled eggs strewn with golden and orange marigold petals.

1 *Boil the eggs by placing them in a pan of boiling water for four minutes. Plunge them in cold water and allow to cool. Shell them carefully and cut into quarters.*

2 *Stir together the curry powder or paste, mayonnaise and cream in a mixing bowl.*

3 *Place the chopped parsley and mixed salad leaves in individual bowls, scatter with the eggs and then pour over the curried cream sauce. Add a generous scattering of marigold petals. Serve as a salad with baked ham and thick wholemeal (whole-wheat) bread.*

Blue Blooms

Right: Anchusa azurea
'Loddon Royalist'.

Anchusa is a tall, hardy plant which is part of the borage family. In a matter of weeks, it will grow as high as 1.5m/5ft, producing large panicles of bright blue flowers. There are several beautiful hybrids to choose from. *Anchusa azurea* 'Loddon Royalist' has deep blue flowers, while 'Opal' is a paler blue. 'Little John' is a dwarf by comparison, growing only 45cm/18in high, but has lovely deep blue flowers.

Anchusa's long flowering period means that it overlaps with sweet rocket (arugula) in early summer and is still flowering when the bergamot blooms. For kitchen purposes, one plant will provide plenty of flowers.

in the garden

Anchusa makes a striking addition to the garden where it will grow happily among other herbaceous perennials at the back of the border. It can also be grown in a large container, perhaps with roses for company. Either way, it will need the support of twigs or canes. Anchusa grows well in either sun or partial shade but it likes to be kept moist during the growing season, particularly in containers. To encourage flower production cut back the upper half of the stems after flowering. New shoots will soon grow and another succession of buds will follow. In the autumn it is best to cut down all the top growth in order to encourage the formation of a sturdy basal rosette of leaves from which the new shoots will grow the following spring. The plant is best kept on the dry side over the winter.

Left: Anchusa grows rather tall in a pot and needs support. After the first flush of flowers, cut the stems down to within 30cm/12in of the ground and they will soon send up new flower shoots. Here it makes a delightful partnership with Rosa 'Lancashire'.

Above: Anchusa makes an excellent cut flower for a vase inside the house. It lasts for a long time in water and provides a good supply of material for the kitchen. By cutting lengthy stems you will encourage further growth.

A nchusa flowers are such a beautiful bright blue that they are a valuable and versatile addition to many food dishes. They look striking set amidst orange and yellow flowers in a salad and are exquisite crystallized with egg white and sugar and used to decorate sponge cakes, roulades, mousses or summer syllabub. How lovely they look, mixed with other crystallized flowers such as alpine pinks and dainty pink rose petals. They can be scattered amongst fruit in a fruit syrup or set in ice cubes for summer drinks. They can be floated over cucumber vinegar and, unlike borage, will not change colour.

Right: Bright blue anchusa flowers make an outstanding garnish.

ANCHUSA, ORANGE AND WATERCRESS SALAD

Anchusa flowers make a delightful decoration on a sliced orange salad. The colours make the dish vibrant and fresh, especially set against the deep green of the watercress, with the dark stain of balsamic vinegar cast over the oranges.

- SERVES 4
- INGREDIENTS
  12 anchusa flowers
  2 seedless oranges
  1 bunch watercress

For the dressing
15ml/1 tbsp balsamic vinegar
60ml/4 tbsp olive oil

1 △ *To prepare the flowers for the salad, remove the flower-head from the green calyx by gently teasing it out. It should come away easily.*

2 △ *Use a sharp knife to peel the oranges and slice horizontally into thin sections. Arrange on a salad plate, surrounded by small sprigs of watercress.*

3 *Scatter the anchusa flowers over the oranges, then drizzle with a mixture of balsamic vinegar and olive oil. Eat with cold duck or pâté and plenty of French bread.*

Pleasing with Pinks

Above: *Alpine pinks can be combined with lavender and violets in a scented hanging basket.*

Many different alpine pinks are available which will be equally at home in pots, hanging baskets or at the front of the flowerbed. They all love a well-drained, sunny site and will provide lots of colour and scent throughout mid-summer. Alpine pinks easily root from cuttings taken in summer and are all hardy, evergreen, neat little plants with single, semi-double or double flowers. Flower varieties are either described as "selfs" which are of one colour; "laced" with a fringe of darker or lighter colouring; "fancies" with stripes, flakes or flecks that are different to the ground colour; or "bicolour" where the central area is of a contrasting hue to the rest of the flower.

in the garden

ALPINE PINK SELECTION BASKET

This pretty wire basket has been painted blue to complement the colours used in the planting scheme. It provides a beautiful background for a simple arrangement of various alpine pinks. There are so many different types to choose from. Either follow the suggestions given in the ingredients or choose your own, depending on availability. If in doubt, read the plant labels very carefully and buy the most scented varieties.

- INGREDIENTS
  1 alpine pink plant *Dianthus* 'Whatfield Can-Can'
  1 alpine pink plant *Dianthus* 'Whatfield Magenta'
  1 alpine pink plant *Dianthus* 'Calypso Star'
  1 alpine pink plant *Dianthus* 'Dainty Dame'

- MOSS
- LINER Black plastic lining from the bottom of a refuse sack (garbage bag), cut generously to fit the depth of the basket
- DRAINAGE Old crocks (china), grit (gravel) or pieces of polystyrene (plastic foam)
- COMPOST (SOIL MIX) Use fresh compost in containers. Choose either a soil-based compost or a proprietary potting compost (planting mix). Although optional it is recommended that you add water-retaining crystals at the

  time of planting
- CONTAINER 33cm/13in diameter wire basket; this one has been painted blue
- SITE Sun or shade
- WHEN TO PLANT Late spring
- AT ITS BEST Early to mid-summer

Below: *Alpine pinks are easily
propagated from strong side
shoots taken in mid-summer.*

1 △ *Cover the base and sides
of the basket with a generous
layer of moss. Cut several
2.5cm/1in slits in the bottom
of the plastic liner to allow
excess moisture to drain away.*

2 △ *Place the plastic liner in
position. Cut off any excess or
leave to tuck in at the end of the
planting. Add a layer of
drainage material and then
enough compost to bring level to
within 5cm/2in of the rim of
the basket.*

3 △ *Arrange the four alpine
pinks around the edge of the
basket. Water well. Firm in the
plants. Add more compost and
moss if necessary.*

in the kitchen

Above: *You can also use crystallized pinks to decorate cookies, secured in place with a little glacé icing.*

The clove-like scent of alpine pinks made them a favourite flower for use in the kitchens of the Middle Ages where they were better known by the name "gillyflower". Another name for them was "sops in wine" on account of their use for flavouring wine. Indeed *Dianthus* 'Sops in Wine' is still available through specialist nurseries.

When using the flowers it was, and still is, common practice to cut off the white heels or ends of the flower petals which retain a bitter flavour. As with rosemary and lavender, in the past a conserve of gillyflowers was made, layering the flowers with sugar. Vinegar was sometimes added to this to make a sweet-flavoured condiment, or simply added to the petals without the sugar. A pickle was made using white wine vinegar, cinnamon, mace and lots of flowers. The pickled petals were then minced with sugar and a little fresh vinegar, rather like the mint sauce of today eaten with lamb.

in the kitchen ## MERINGUES WITH CRYSTALLIZED PINKS

One of the easiest ways to use pinks is to crystallize a few of the flowers and then add them to meringues, cakes or ice creams. You could try substituting rose- or alpine pink-flavoured sugar (*see* Using flowers), instead of ordinary sugar in the meringues.

- MAKES ABOUT 14
- INGREDIENTS
  4 egg whites
  225g/8oz icing (confectioners') sugar (or lavender or alpine pink sugar)
  10ml/2 tsp vanilla extract (if using plain icing sugar)

  For the filling
  300ml/½ pint/1¼ cups double (heavy) cream

- TO DECORATE
  40–50 crystallized alpine pink petals, white heel removed (these should be made one or two days before serving them)

1 *Preheat the oven to 120ºC/ 250ºF/Gas ½. Line two baking sheets with parchment paper. Whisk the egg whites in a large bowl until stiff. Add the sugar, a tablespoonful at a time, until the mixture is stiff and glossy. Stir in the vanilla.*

2 △ *Place large spoonfuls of the meringue, spaced well apart, on the baking sheets. Shape into little nests by making a cavity in the centre of each with the back of a teaspoon. Bake for about 1¼ hours or until the meringues are crisp. Leave to cool.*

3 △ *Whip the cream until just holding its shape and spoon into the nests. Scatter the crystallized petals over the meringues just before serving.*

Aromatic Thyme

There is a wide variety of thymes to choose from, all of which enjoy dry, sunny conditions. The leaves are especially aromatic and the flowers taste just like the foliage, only sweeter. The lemon-scented thymes are particularly pleasing, but then so, too, are the orange-scented and caraway thyme varieties. Grow them between warm paving stones on a sunny terrace (they love alkaline soils) or patio, or plant them in a special raised bed. Mix them with other herbs in hanging baskets, try them in shallow wooden containers or grow them in pots. They easily strike from cuttings and can also be grown from seed.

Right: Thyme plants create a wonderful flowering front to a summer herb basket.

in the garden

FLOWERING BOUQUET GARNI

This is a medium-sized terracotta pot planted with two variegated lemon-scented thymes, various parsleys and a taller bay – all the ingredients necessary for a bouquet garni.

- INGREDIENTS
  1 bay *Laurus nobilis* (you could use a standard bay)
  2 thyme plants *Thymus x citriodorus* 'Aureus'
  3 parsley plants *Petroselinum crispum*, one is the flat-leaf French or Italian parsley *P.c.* var. *neapolitanum*

- DRAINAGE Old crocks (china), grit (gravel) or pieces of polystyrene (plastic foam)
- COMPOST (SOIL MIX) Choose a soil-based compost or a proprietary potting compost (planting mix) with added water-retaining crystals

- CONTAINER Use a medium to large pot depending on the size of the bay. This pot is 30cm/12in diameter and 27.5cm/11in deep
- SITE Sunny
- WHEN TO PLANT Early spring
- AT ITS BEST Mid-summer to autumn

1 *Prepare the container for planting by covering the base with 5cm/2in drainage material. Add compost to a depth of about 5cm/2in. Plant the bay at the back of the pot and add a little more compost.*

2 *Plant the thymes on either side of the bay. Then plant one parsley at the centre front with the other two beyond the thymes near the edge of the pot.*

3 *Fill in gaps with compost. Water well. Firm in the plants and add more compost if necessary.*

AFTERCARE
Keep the compost moist at all times. Once the parsley is established it can be picked regularly. Gather the bay and parsley leaves as you require them. Trim off thyme flowers as soon as they are past their best and cut the stems to half their original length, in order to encourage a neat overall shape. This is a long-term planting scheme for the thyme and the bay tree.

in the kitchen

Right: Bay, parsley and thyme create a powerful ensemble to flavour many dishes.

Thyme will begin to flower in early summer in various shades of pink. The tiny blooms appear either in dense clusters at the end of the leaf stems or as individual flowers at leaf joints along the stem. Pick only the freshest blooms for use in the kitchen. Use them to flavour soups, pâtés, salads, pastas, butter and oils. They have lots of zingy, often lemony, flavour and can be used wherever you want to add extra punch to your cooking.

in the kitchen

PROVENÇAL THYME MUSHROOMS

Here, thyme flowers have been added to roasted mushrooms topped with breadcrumbs. The result is an aromatic taste of the Mediterranean.

- SERVES 8
- INGREDIENTS

  8 large mushrooms

  120ml/8 tbsp white breadcrumbs

  30ml/2 tbsp thyme leaves

  2 cloves garlic

  30ml/2 tbsp thyme flowers

  coarse salt and freshly ground black pepper

  45ml/3 tbsp olive oil

1 *Clean and skin the mushrooms. Remove and chop the stalks. Place the mushrooms cup side up on a large ovenproof dish.*

2 *Blend the bread, mushroom stalks, thyme leaves and garlic in a food processor. Add plenty of salt and pepper, and 15ml/1 tbsp olive oil. Then mix in 15ml/1 tbsp thyme flowers.*

3 *Divide the bread mixture between the mushrooms and drizzle over the remaining olive oil.*

4 *Cook in a hot oven until the mushrooms are soft and the breadcrumbs lightly browned. Scatter over the remaining flowers just before serving.*

FRESH BOUQUET GARNI
Make little posies with a few bay leaves, a few parsley leaves and some thyme flowers to use for making stock or for flavouring a white fish sauce. These plants are evergreen, so you should be able to gather fresh leaves throughout the year whenever you need them. In the early summer you will have the benefit of the thyme flowers as well as the leaves.

Flavour of the Moment

Right: Sage flowers have such a good flavour and are so prolifically produced that they should be used for lots of different dishes including salads, butter and sauces.

Sage produces a mass of brilliant flowers in mid-summer and every flower is full of flavour, tasting like a mild version of the leaf. There are several different types of culinary sage. Some have narrow grey leaves, others have golden variegated leaves. Purple, or red, sage has a dusky purple colouring. Tricolour sage is a variegated form that is not quite hardy. All forms produce edible flowers in shades of blue, some with a more purple tinge. Each one is tasty and equally good in the kitchen.

There are tender sages such as *Salvia elegans* 'Scarlet Pineapple' with its pineapple-scented leaves and long, tubular red flowers. These are packed with gorgeous colour and a lovely flavour. Clary sage, *Salvia sclarea*, also produces flowers that are good to eat.

in the garden

SAGE AND GARLIC CHIVE POT

This pot provides an interesting collection of hardy sages each with different coloured leaves, yet all producing beautiful flowers in various shades of blue in mid-summer. Spiky Chinese chives are planted between each sage, each leaf tasting mildly of garlic, and usable in lots of ways.

- INGREDIENTS
  1 broad-leaf sage plant *Salvia officinalis* 'Broad Leaf'
  1 golden variegated sage plant *Salvia officinalis* 'Icterina'
  1 purple- (or red-) leaf sage plant *Salvia officinalis* 'Purpurea'
  3 garlic chive plants *Allium tuberosum*

- DRAINAGE Old crocks (china), grit (gravel) or small pieces of polystyrene (plastic foam)
- COMPOST (SOIL MIX) Use fresh compost in containers. Choose either a soil-based compost or a proprietary potting compost (planting mix). Add water-retaining crystals at the time of planting
- CONTAINER Large pot

38cm/15in diameter and 25cm/10in deep or use a wooden half barrel
- SITE Full sun
- WHEN TO PLANT Early spring to mid-summer
- AT ITS BEST Mid-summer to autumn

1 *Cover the base of the container with 5cm/2in drainage material and add about 8–10cm/3–4in compost.*

2 *Plant the three sage plants around the edge of the container with a pot of garlic chives between each one.*

3 *Fill in any gaps with compost, bringing the compost level to within 2.5cm/1in from the top of the container. Water well. Firm in the plants and add more compost if necessary.*

AFTERCARE
Keep the compost moist during the growing season but drier during the winter months. If the pot does not flower the first year, it will the second. Harvest the flowers for the kitchen, and then cut off all flower spikes after the sage has completed its flowering. Early the following spring, prune all the sages back by one third. If possible transfer the contents to a larger pot.

in the kitchen

*Right: The long, tubular
flowers of all sages are
surprisingly tasty.*

The sage family is a very large one and produces many culinary treats including flavouring for oils, vinegars, butters, salads and cold sauces.

In the 17th century, recipes recorded how sage flowers were mixed with white wine or water, and then distilled to make sage water. The flowers were also beaten with sugar and kept in a glass jar to make a "conserve of sage".

Clary sage flowers were special favourites for strewing on salads, adding to soups and making clary wine which was renowned for its narcotic properties.

in the kitchen ## SAGE-FLOWER MUSTARD

This creamy sauce has a mild mustardy flavour which looks and tastes wonderful with the addition of the sage flowers. At the height of summer, it makes a simple but punchy partner for barbecued sausages. Strengthen or weaken the sage flavour to suit your own taste.

- SERVES 4
- INGREDIENTS

30ml/2 tbsp sage flowers, all
  green parts removed
60ml/4 tbsp crème fraîche
1ml/¼ tsp English mustard
  powder
15ml/1 tbsp young sage
  leaves
15ml/1 tbsp garlic chive
  leaves

1 △ *Carefully pull each sage flower out of its socket. Discard any that are damaged.*

2 *In a medium bowl combine the crème fraîche and mustard powder.*

3 △ *Finely shred and cut the sage leaves and garlic chive leaves into very small segments and add to the mixture.*

4 *Toss lightly together and add the sage flowers. Serve with barbecued sausages, green salad and crispy rolls.*

COOK'S TIP
Sage flowers lose their beautiful colouring when cooked. They turn brown.

Citrus Scents

Lemon verbena is a deciduous shrub from Chile and Argentina where it grows up to 3m/10ft high. It has one of the most powerfully scented of all leaves – just one touch will leave the aroma lingering for quite a while. It will be killed by frost in all but the mildest of gardens so it is best kept in a pot and overwintered in a greenhouse where even the dry leaves are marvellously scented. Keep it fairly dry throughout the winter months, then water more in the spring when the new leaves start to appear. Prune in spring to keep the plant in good shape. It will eventually reach 90cm–1.2m (3–4ft).

Left: Lemon verbena flowers are tiny but, like the leaves, are packed with the flavour of lemon.

in the garden   ORANGES AND LEMONS

This is a window-box packed with aromatic leaves. Here orange- and lemon-scented geraniums make an attractive partnership with lemon verbena.

- INGREDIENTS
  1 scented geranium plant
  Pelargonium 'Prince of Orange'
  1 scented geranium plant
  Pelargonium crispum 'Variegatum'
  1 lemon verbena plant
  Aloysia triphylla

- DRAINAGE Old crocks (china), grit (gravel) or pieces of polystyrene (plastic foam)
- COMPOST (SOIL MIX) Use either a soil-based compost or a proprietary potting compost (planting mix). Add water-retaining crystals
- CONTAINER Window-box, 40cm/16in long by 15cm/6in wide and deep
- SITE In a conservatory or greenhouse until early summer, then move outside to a sunny sheltered spot
- WHEN TO PLANT Early summer
- AT ITS BEST Summer to autumn

1 △ *Cover the base of the container with 2.5cm/1in of drainage material and add 5cm/2in of compost.*

2 △ *Plant the variegated geranium at one end of the box, with the lemon verbena in the centre and the orange-scented geranium at the other end. Add enough compost to bring level to within 2.5cm/1in of the rim. Water well and firm the plants.*

AFTERCARE
Keep the compost moist from late spring through the summer. It should be left drier throughout the cooler days of winter. Use or remove all flowers to promote further flower production. Overwinter in a greenhouse or conservatory. Pot into a bigger container the following year.

in the kitchen

Right: Once the flowers are picked they do not stay fresh very long, so pick them to use only shortly before you serve.

Both the flowers and leaves of lemon verbena have a strong lemon flavour and can be used in drinks, ice creams and jellies. Use the leaves at the bottom of sponge cakes to give flavour to the cake mixture, then remove them after cooking. Dried or powdered, they can be added to many different stuffings, as well as fish cakes and herb dumplings. The leaves and flowers could also be used to make scented oils and vinegars. Dry leaves make an excellent addition to pot-pourri. Treat scented geranium leaves in the same way.

in the kitchen

APPLE SNOW WITH LEMON VERBENA

The recipe uses lemon verbena leaves to impart the flavour of lemon, while the delicate flowers are used to decorate the top.

- SERVES 4
- INGREDIENTS
  450g/1lb cooking apples, peeled and cored
  50g/2oz caster (superfine) sugar
  30ml/2 tbsp water
  16 young lemon verbena leaves
  2 egg whites

- TO DECORATE
  4–8 young lemon verbena leaves
  4 sprays lemon verbena flowers

1 *Slice the apples and add them to a pan with the sugar, water and lemon verbena leaves. Cover and simmer gently for 10–15 minutes. Put through a sieve (strainer) to extract the leaves and make a smooth purée, then leave to cool.*

2 *Whisk the egg whites until stiff and fold in the apple purée.*

3 *Spoon into glasses and decorate with a sprinkling of lemon verbena flowers and perhaps one or two small leaves dusted with egg white and sugar.*

COOK'S TIP
If you have any leftovers, fold whipped cream into the mixture and freeze. Use as a delicious ice cream and sprinkle on the lemon verbena flowers when just about to serve.

Geranium Inspirations

Right: 'Attar of Roses' has delightful rose-scented leaves with a pretty pale pink flower.

Left: 'Capitatum' has scented leaves and a beautiful rich pink flower.

Scented geraniums are renowned for their fragrant leaves. Lemon-, spice-, peppermint- and orange-scented varieties all exist, and they are all surprisingly powerful, but one of the loveliest is the 'Attar of Roses' variety, which has soft, downy, rose-scented leaves. Scented geranium flowers vary in colour and size with 'Attar of Roses' being small and a pretty, pale pink, while 'Capitatum' is much larger and bright pink. 'Prince of Orange' has exquisite maroon markings on its lilac-pink petals and *P. crispum* 'Variegatum', although shy to flower, has pale mauve clusters with wonderfully lemon-scented leaves. These are just some of the many varieties available.

Scented geraniums will be killed by frost so they need the protection of a greenhouse or windowsill indoors through the winter. They should be kept fairly dry during this period. In summer, they can remain indoors or be planted in pots outside. Take cuttings of non-flowering shoots in spring or autumn.

in the garden · SCENTED GERANIUM POT

Tender geraniums 'Attar of Roses' and 'Capitatum' share this pot with a mature lemon verbena plant which has been potted on several times.

- **INGREDIENTS**
  1 lemon verbena plant
  Aloysia tryphylla
  1 scented geranium plant
  Pelargonium 'Attar of Roses'
  1 scented geranium plant
  Pelargonium 'Capitatum'

- **DRAINAGE** Old crocks (china), grit (gravel) or small pieces of polystyrene (plastic foam)
- **COMPOST (SOIL MIX)** Use fresh compost in containers. Choose either a soil-based

compost or a proprietary potting compost (planting mix). Water-retaining crystals can be added at time of planting
- **CONTAINER** Pot 40cm/16in wide by 30cm/12in deep
- **SITE** In a conservatory or greenhouse until early summer, then move outside to a sunny sheltered spot
- **WHEN TO PLANT** Early summer
- **AT ITS BEST** Mid-summer to autumn

1 *Cover the base of the container with 5cm/2in of drainage material and add about 20cm/8in of compost.*

2 *Plant the lemon verbena towards the centre back with the geraniums to the front on either side.*

3 *Add enough compost to bring level to within 2.5cm/1in of the rim. Water well and firm the plants.*

AFTERCARE
Keep the compost moist from late spring and through the summer. It should be left drier throughout the cooler days of winter. Use or remove all flowers to promote further flower production. Overwinter in a greenhouse or conservatory. Pot into a bigger container every two years. Prune back the lemon verbena and geraniums every spring. They can all be cut back hard and will soon sprout again.

Left: A scented geranium pot adds colour and aroma to the corner of a courtyard.

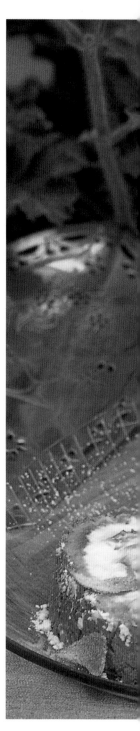

in the kitchen

Scented geraniums are one of the few examples of plants in this book where the leaves are more powerfully scented than the flowers. As a result, the flowers are used more for their colour in this recipe. However, the flowers will look fabulous crystallized on meringues, roulades and biscuits. They also look exquisite in ice cubes and in ice bowls.

ROSE GERANIUM ROULADE

The recipe uses 'Attar of Roses' leaves to give flavour to the roulade itself while using the colour of 'Capitatum' petals for the decoration.

- SERVES 6
- INGREDIENTS
  12–16 young 'Attar of Roses' geranium leaves
  5 medium eggs, separated
  275g/10oz caster (superfine) sugar

30ml/2 tbsp icing (confectioners') sugar, plus extra for dusting
300ml/½ pint/1¼ cups double (heavy) cream
a few drops of rose-water
2 kiwi fruit

10–15 fresh or crystallized 'Capitatum' geranium petals

1 △ *Preheat the oven to 180ºC/350ºF/Gas 4. Line a 20cm x 27.5cm/8 x 11in baking tray with baking parchment and lay the geranium leaves all over it.*

2 *Beat together the egg yolks and sugar until light and fluffy.*

3 *In a separate bowl, whisk the egg white until stiff and then fold into the egg yolk and sugar mixture until it is smooth.*

4 *Pour the mixture on top of the geranium leaves and bake for about 10 minutes until just set.*

5 *Remove from the oven and leave to cool.*

6 *Turn the roulade out on to a clean piece of baking parchment dusted with icing sugar. Carefully remove the geranium leaves.*

7 *Add a few drops of rose-water to the cream and then whip until soft peaks form.*

8 *Spread the whipped cream over the roulade. Peel and thinly slice the kiwi fruit and distribute over the surface of the cream.*

9 △ *Roll up the roulade, holding the long edges. Dust with icing sugar and arrange fresh petals on top. This recipe will work equally well with crystallized petals.*

One Day at a Time

D ay lilies are native to the marshy river valleys and meadowlands of Japan, China and Korea. Most flowers last for just one day, hence their name. They open in the afternoon and remain open through the night, but there is such a succession of blooms that the flowering period usually lasts for several weeks. The colours of the flowers range from cream, yellow and orange, to pink, dark purple and almost black. Orange flowers are the most common and *Hemerocallis fulva*, with its tawny-orange petals, is a particularly fine example.

Left: *Day lilies are very easy to grow and one plant will multiply to produce a large clump.*

in the garden The plants form large clumps in the garden, sometimes 1m/3ft tall by 1.2m/4ft across. They like a moist soil in a sunny position. There are many dwarf hybrids available which are suitable for containers.

Above: *Tiger lilies* (Lilium lancifolium) *have long been a favourite flower in Chinese cooking. 'Enchantment' can be substituted. Here it is seen growing with red orache* Atriplex hortensis.

Right: Hemerocallis fulva *'Europa' derives from one of the main species of day lily with tawny-orange flowers, each with a yellow base.*

in the kitchen

Right: Day lily flowers and buds have a distinctive flavour, like peppery mangetouts (snow peas).

ay lilies have been used in Chinese cooking for centuries. Both the buds and petals can be eaten. They have a delicious crunchy texture and the flavour of mangetouts (snow peas) with a peppery aftertaste. They are excellent cooked in stir-fries, added to pastas or used fresh on salads. The recipe below uses the petals cooked in a quick stir-fry, with additional fresh petals strewn over the finished dish as a garnish.

in the kitchen

STIR-FRIED DUCK WITH DAY LILIES

The flavour of day lilies combined with a hint of ginger make this a delicious way to serve duck.

• SERVES 4–6

• INGREDIENTS

450g/1lb lean duck breast
1 garlic clove, crushed
2 slices root ginger, shredded
45ml/3 tbsp vegetable oil
4 spring onions (scallions),
    sliced lengthways
20 day lily buds, halved
    lengthways
45ml/3 tbsp soy sauce
30ml/2 tbsp sherry
petals of 4 day lilies
10ml/2 tsp cornflour
    (cornstarch)
noodles, to serve

• TO GARNISH
2 day lilies

COOK'S TIP
Because day lilies only open in the afternoon you may want to trick them into opening in the morning. Cut stems with fat buds, and keep them in the refrigerator over night. The next day, put the stems into hot water and watch them open.

1 *Cut the duck into small pieces and place in a bowl with the garlic and ginger. Pour over 15ml/1 tbsp of oil and leave to marinate for 30 minutes.*

2 *Heat the remaining oil in a wok or a deep frying pan. Add the spring onions and day lily buds and stir-fry for 30 seconds.*

3 *Add the duck pieces with the garlic and ginger and cook for 2 minutes.*

4 *Add the soy sauce, sherry and day lily petals and cook for 2 minutes. Blend the cornflour with 15ml/ 1 tbsp water and stir into the pan. Cook for 1 minute, stirring until thickened.*

5 *Garnish with fresh day lily petals and serve with noodles.*

A Traditional Flowery Treat

Right: The scent of freshly opened elderflowers is reminiscent of muscat grapes.

The elder is native to northern Europe where it is extremely common. It grows very easily from seed which is often dispersed by birds. Indeed, it often appears in the most surprising places, being recognized by its strong smelling leaves when crushed. Fortunately, the roots of the elder are easily removed when young, although less easily after the first year.

The elder is certainly of great value to the kitchen, both in the summer when it is smothered with creamy flowers, and in the autumn when its fruits are a luscious dark purple. The fruit must never be eaten if it is unripe, and when ripe, only after cooking.

in the garden

Once established, the elder can be cut right down to the ground and it will soon sprout up again. However, in the right place it is a beautiful tree attaining a height and spread of 6m/20ft. Various forms exist including 'Aurea' with its golden leaves, and 'Guincho Purple'.

Right: Throughout northern Europe, Scandinavia and Russia there are many folk tales about the elder, many associated with witchcraft. In England it was believed that if you planted an elder in the herb garden and stood beneath it at midnight on Midsummer's eve, you would see the King of the Elves pass by with his entourage.

in the kitchen

Right: Afternoon tea is all the more memorable for its delicious scones and fragrant elderflower and strawberry jam.

Elderflowers have a heady, musky scent and it is this fragrance that has made the elderflower such a popular ingredient of hot and cold drinks. Elderflower cordial, elderflower tea and heady elderflower champagne have all been made for generations, with elderflower cordial regaining popularity in recent years and now readily available in supermarkets. Choose only the freshest flowers for use in the kitchen, just as they are beginning to open, when their flavour is at its best. Shake off any insects or plunge the flower-heads into salty water.

in the kitchen ## ELDERFLOWER AND STRAWBERRY JAM

The heady scent of elderflowers is captured in this strawberry jam, making a wonderfully fragrant conserve for use with scones and cream on a summer's afternoon. In the depths of winter the fragrance will evoke the balmy days of summer.

- MAKES ABOUT 4.5KG/10LB
- INGREDIENTS
    8 elderflower heads
        with newly opened flowers
    3.2kg/7lb strawberries
    juice of 2 lemons
    2.7kg/6lb sugar

OTHER CULINARY USES

Try elderflower and peppermint tea which is simply made by pouring 850ml/1½ pint/3¾ cups of boiling water on 3 or 4 heads of elderflowers and a small handful of peppermint.

Elderflower is used as a flavouring with many fruits including strawberries, gooseberries and rhubarb and may be used in the making of jams and fruit pies. It adds a wonderful musky fragrance and flavour and is certainly well worth trying.

1 *Cut the elderflowers off the main stem and tie the florets in a muslin (cheesecloth) bag.*

2 *Hull the strawberries and then mash with the lemon juice. Put in a preserving pan with the elderflowers in muslin.*

3 *Simmer until the fruit is soft, stirring frequently to prevent burning.*

4 *Add the sugar, stirring until it is all dissolved. Boil rapidly until setting point is reached. To test for setting, pour a small spoonful in a saucer and leave to cool. If a wrinkle forms on the top when pushed with a finger the jam will set.*

5 *With a slotted spoon, remove the elderflowers and any scum that has formed. Leave to cool.*

6 *Stir and pour into prepared sterilized jars. Cover and label. Once opened, keep in the refrigerator and consume within a week.*

Summer Favourite

Right: The distinctive sky-blue star of the borage flower was a popular motif in medieval tapestries and needlepoint.

The sky-blue, star-shaped borage flower is eye-catching in its own right; the newly opened flowers taste of fresh cucumber, especially when eaten with the black centre and sweetly flavoured nectar. The stems have a high water content, and can be peeled and used like cucumber – in the past, when cucumber were available only to those with greenhouses, borage stems were often used as a substitute. Borage is an ancient plant and has been used in cooking for centuries. It is believed to have been brought to Britain by the Romans. Although the petals are usually blue, occasionally they can be pink and sometimes even white.

in the garden

Borage is a hardy annual which will self-seed, or grow from seed sown in the spring. It grows quickly in the early summer months and by mid-summer may be 60cm/2ft high by 45cm/18in across. It is easily grown in a sunny part of the garden and can be planted among pink roses and many herbaceous plants. It is equally attractive in the herb garden with bergamot and sage for company.

Borage can also be grown in containers, although the containers will need to be large to accommodate this plant. A wooden half barrel or large terracotta pot would be ideal. Either put two or three borage plants in the same container, or use a single plant as a centrepiece with smaller supporting herbs around it. A partnership of mint and lemon balm would make the perfect combination to flavour a summer punch. It might be necessary to use twig supports to help keep the borage upright as it can grow rather leggy in containers.

Left: Why not sow an edible flower garden where borage can have courgettes (zucchini), nasturtiums and sunflowers for company? Two or three borage plants will be sufficient for kitchen use, but they are so easy to grow and look so pretty that more will always be welcome.

in the kitchen

Right: Borage flowers are among the prettiest of the edible flowers.

Borage flowers are so elegant and distinctive and are such a gorgeous blue that for their appearance alone they are a welcome addition to many food dishes. Their star-like qualities will be enjoyed everywhere.

Their central black stamens look particularly striking and the flowers look wonderful as crystallized decorations on cakes, mousses or other desserts. The colours work well alongside other crystallized flowers such as alpine pinks and rose petals. Alternatively scatter them amongst fruit, or set in ice cubes for summer drinks.

in the kitchen

SUMMER PUNCH

Summertime means a long, cool drink and a lazy afternoon. The beautiful borage flowers add the final essential ingredient. Here, the tastes of cucumber and mint are complemented by the flavour of the borage flower.

- Serves 4–6
- Ingredients
  several sprigs of borage
  ¼ cucumber
  1 small orange
  ¼ bottle Pimm's, chilled
  several sprigs of mint and/or
  lemon balm
  ice cubes
  1 bottle lemonade (lemon soda), ginger beer or ginger ale

1 △ *To prepare the flowers, remove each flower-head from the green calyx by gently teasing it out. It should come away easily.*

2 △ *Halve the cucumber lengthways, then cut into thin slices. Chop the orange into small chunks, leaving the skin on. Put in a large jug (pitcher) and add the Pimm's, mint and/or lemon balm, followed by the borage and ice cubes. Mix in the lemonade, ginger beer or ginger ale, stirring gently. Serve in tall glasses with flowers on top of each glass.*

summer favourite

This is very much a help-yourself and do-it-yourself fruit salad, where the fruit is shown off in all its beauty. The summer berries look sumptuous with a river of raspberry purée running through, topped by bright blue borage flowers. This is an idea which lends itself to many interpretations. It can be kept very simple, using just two types of fruit, or wonderfully luxurious as seen here.

Left: Borage has a long flowering period which means that it is available to use with lots of summer fruits from early strawberries and raspberries to peaches and apricots later in the season.

- SERVES 6–8
- INGREDIENTS
  3–4 passion fruit
  half a melon
  350g/12oz strawberries
  115g/4oz cherries
  100g/3½oz blueberries
  115g/4oz raspberries
  12–15 borage flowers
  For the purée
  225g/8oz raspberries
  15ml/1 tbsp icing
    (confectioners') sugar

- TO SERVE
  caster (superfine) sugar and
    softly whipped cream

1 *Prepare the fruit. Cut the passion fruit in half. Make melon balls if you have a melon baller, otherwise just cut into chunks. Slice a few strawberries in half, leaving the rest whole with their green calyx intact. The cherries can be left with their stalks, if desired. The blueberries and raspberries should be left whole.*

If you prefer, you can easily remove the strawberry calyxes and cherry stalks, and scoop the passion fruit flesh from the skin before serving the fruit salad.

2 △ *For the purée, press the raspberries through a sieve (strainer) into a bowl to extract the seeds. Stir in the icing sugar, adding a little more if necessary to sweeten.*

3 △ *Arrange the fruit on a large serving plate, leaving the middle of the plate clear. Spoon the raspberry purée down the centre of the platter, through the berries and melon. Chill until ready to serve.*

4 *Just before serving arrange the borage flowers over the purée. Offer caster sugar and softly whipped cream at the table.*

The Versatile Rose

Right: 'William Lobb' has a fringe of moss around the base of its flowers which gives it an apple scent.

Left: 'Gertrude Jekyll' is a popular rose for both its scent and colour. It is ideal for the garden and for a large container.

Below: 'Rosa Mundi' is one of the oldest roses, dating back to the 16th century.

In order to make successful preparations in the kitchen with rose petals, it is essential to grow sweetly scented varieties. There are a great many to choose from including nearly all the old-fashioned roses with their full petals and sweet perfume such as the pink-and-white striped 'Rosa Mundi'; moss roses including 'William Lobb' with its magenta pink flowers; and Bourbon roses such as pink 'Louise Odier' and deeper pink 'Mme Isaac Pereire', both of which flower from mid-summer to mid-autumn. The climber 'Cecile Brunner' is exceptional for its pale pink scroll-like buds, which are perfect for crystallizing whole. Other climbers such as dark red 'Guinée' and pink 'Zéphirine Drouhin' are to be recommended as well. Many of David Austin's breed of English roses are highly scented, including pink 'Mary Rose', apricot 'Evelyn', deep purple 'The Prince' and rich pink, gloriously scented 'Gertrude Jekyll'. Neat little 'Cambridgeshire' is a vibrant mix of pinky-red and yellow and looks lovely scattered on a bowl of strawberries. These are just a few favourites but there are scores of others besides.

in the garden   All the sweetly scented rose varieties mentioned opposite can be grown among other plants such as lavender, sage and hyssop in a herb bed, while in a cottage garden they combine beautifully with borage, rosemary and sweet rocket (arugula). They can all be grown in containers.

Grow climbers and shrub roses in deep barrels with marjoram, lavender, dianthus or rosemary for partners. Use a shrub, tree and rose compost (soil mix) to allow for the long-term nature of the container. The soil needs to be kept moist at all times.

Left: 'Louise Odier', like all other roses, is a heavy feeder and will respond well to a generous mulch and feed in early spring and again in mid-summer. Remember to remove fading heads from all the repeat flowerers in order to encourage further production.

Below: 'Cambridgeshire ' is one of the new 'County Series' of roses. It has very sweet scented flowers which appear from mid-summer to mid-winter.

Below: Gather the flowers on a dry morning using only the freshest, most scented varieties in the kitchen.

in the kitchen

Right: *This glorious cake is filled with a fragrant filling of rose-petal butter cream while the top has been decorated with beautiful crystallized roses.*

Throughout history, the rose has been used in a wide range of sweet recipes. Rose-water, rose-flavoured honey, rose oil, rose candies, rose sugar, rose-petal jam, rose-petal jelly and rose butter are just some of its uses.

Crystallized roses, either petals or whole flowers, are exquisite, and will lift cakes, frozen desserts or light fruit mousses into the realm of the truly spectacular. The rose-scented sorbet below is decorated with a crown of whole crystallized roses.

in the kitchen

ROSE-PETAL SORBET

WITH CRYSTALLIZED ROSE PETALS

This sorbet makes a wonderful end to a summer meal with its fabulous flavour of roses. Remember to use the most scented variety you can find in the garden. Pick fresh blooms which are newly opened, ideally in the late morning, before the heat of the day evaporates the essential oils.

- SERVES 4–6
- INGREDIENTS
  115g/4oz caster (superfine) sugar
  300ml/½ pint/1¼ cups boiling water
  petals of 3 large, scented red or deep pink roses, white ends of petals removed
  juice of 2 lemons
  300ml/½ pint/1¼ cups rosé wine

- TO DECORATE
  whole crystallized roses or rose petals

1 *Place the sugar in a bowl and add the boiling water. Stir until the sugar has completely dissolved. Add the rose petals and leave to cool completely.*

2 △ *Blend the mixture in a food processor then strain through a sieve (strainer). Add the lemon juice and wine and pour into a freezer container. Freeze for several hours until the mixture has frozen around the edges.*

3 △ *Turn the sorbet into a mixing bowl and whisk until smooth. Re-freeze until frozen around the edges. Repeat the whisking and freezing process once or twice more, until the sorbet is pale and smooth. Freeze until firm.*

4 △ *Serve decorated with crystallized roses or rose petals.*

COOK'S TIP

This sorbet can also be made in an ice cream maker. Churn until firm with a good texture. If the sorbet is too hard, transfer it to the refrigerator for 30 minutes before serving.

For a stunning presentation idea, scoop the sorbet into a rose ice bowl. The bowl and sorbet can be left in the freezer until needed.

Soothing Lavender

Right: *Lavender is an evergreen herb bursting with scent and flavour that grows well with roses and many other beautiful summer-flowering plants. It can also be grown in hanging baskets, pots and other containers.*

Lavender is native to a wide region surrounding the Mediterranean and stretching as far as southwest Asia and India. Several different varieties are available, including deep purple 'Hidcote' which grows 60cm/24in high and 'Jean Davis' which is the same height but with pink flowers. Soft pink 'Loddon Pink' and blue-purple 'Munstead' are both a little more compact at 45cm/18in and would be better for a hanging-basket scheme while taller varieties are best used in pots.

Lavender makes a popular garden plant either for edging a path or border, or planting among roses and other cottage garden plants. It flowers in mid-summer and often again in the autumn.

in the garden

SUMMER FLOWER BASKET

This is a magnificent summer hanging basket with a long period of flowering, from the moment the first violas, thymes and little alpine pinks come into bloom in mid-summer until the lavender comes into its second flowering in early autumn. It is a glorious mix of pinks, blues, white and black, softened by variegated mints and frilly green parsley, with the combination of scents from the plants making it a particular pleasure. A wide range of all these plants is available, which allows for infinite variations depending on individual preferences for colour and taste. If in doubt, read the plant labels very carefully and buy the most scented variety. Just remember to plant the mints near the bottom and the lavender in the top. The rest is up to you!

- INGREDIENTS
  2 eau de cologne mint plants
  Mentha x piperata f. citrata
  1 variegated apple mint plant
  Mentha suaveolens
  'Variegata'
  2 variegated thyme plants
  Thymus x 'Doone Valley'
  1 thyme plant *Thymus*
  'Peter Davies'
  1 lemon thyme plant *Thymus x*
  citriodorus
  1 viola plant *Viola* 'Molly
  Sanderson'
  2 viola plants *Viola* 'Rebecca'
  1 viola plant *Viola* 'White
  Mrs Lancaster'
  2 parsley plants *Petroselinum*
  crispum
  2 alpine pink plants *Dianthus*
  'Whatfield Can-Can'
  2 alpine pink plants *Dianthus*
  'Betty Norton'
  1 lavender plant *Lavendula*
  angustifolia 'Munstead'

- MOSS
- LINER Circle of plastic
  sheeting (cut from the compost
  bag), about the size of a
  tea plate
- COMPOST (SOIL MIX) Choose
  either a soil-based compost or
  a proprietary potting compost
  (planting mix). Add water-
  retaining crystals to the
  compost before or during
  the planting
- CONTAINER 35cm/14in
  diameter wire hanging basket
- SITE Sunny and sheltered
- WHEN TO PLANT Late spring
- AT ITS BEST Early to
  late summer

1 △ *Cover the base and the first third of the sides of the basket with a generous layer of moss. Cover with the circle of plastic sheeting and add a thin layer of compost.*

2 △ *Plant the bottom layer of herbs through the sides of the basket with the eau de cologne mints spaced 10–12cm/4–5in on either side of the central variegated apple mint. This method assumes the basket will hang against a wall and that the back therefore has fewer plants.*

3 △ *Plant two violas, here
'Rebecca' has been used, to grow
either side of the central
variegated mint. Make sure all
the roots have good contact with
the compost.*

4 △ *Add a collar of moss
around each plant and bring
the wall of moss about two-
thirds of the way up the sides of
the basket. Add another
5cm/2in of compost.*

5 △ *Create an upper tier of
herbs, using one of the thymes
for the central position above
the variegated mint, flanked by
two alpine pinks, two parsley
plants and two variegated
thymes. The exact positions are
not crucial; space them so the
end result is balanced. Bring the
wall of moss 2.5cm/1in above
the rim of the basket.*

6 △ *Now in the top, plant the
lavender in the centre back
position. Plant the last two
alpine pinks and violas on
either side at the front, with the
remaining thyme in the middle.
Fill in any gaps with compost.
Water well. Firm in the plants.
Add more compost and moss
if necessary.*

in the kitchen

Lavender flowers are suitable for all sorts of uses in both sweet and savoury dishes. The taste is reminiscent of rosemary, which is why many old recipes are similar to those using rosemary flowers. Old receipt books describe the making of lavender wine, lavender water and lavender tea.

In the 17th century, the flowers were used to make lavender sugar or "a conserve of the flowers of lavender" as it was described in *The Queen's Closet Opened* (1655). "Take the flowers being new as you please, and beat them with three times their weight of White Sugar, after the same manner as Rosemary flowers; they will keep one year." For contemporary purposes a food processor may be used. Let it stand for a week, before using a sieve (strainer) to remove the flower petals.

Right: *Pull lavender flowers off the stem with the blue parts still attached to use in making lavender bread or scones.*

in the kitchen

LAVENDER CHICKEN

Here, lavender flowers are used to perfume and flavour chicken cooked in a large casserole dish with red wine, oranges and thyme. When the lid is removed after cooking, the heady aroma will entice as much as the delicious flavour.

- SERVES **4**
- INGREDIENTS

15ml/1 tbsp butter
15ml/1 tbsp olive oil
8 chicken pieces
8 shallots
30ml/2 tbsp flour
225ml/8fl oz/1 cup red wine
225ml/8fl oz/1 cup chicken
  stock
salt and ground black pepper
4 sprigs thyme
10ml/2 tsp thyme flowers,
  removed from stalk

10ml/2 tsp lavender
  flowers
grated zest and juice of one
  orange

- TO GARNISH

1 orange, divided into
  segments
12 lavender sprigs
20ml/4 tsp lavender flowers

1 *Heat the butter and olive oil in a heavy pan and add the chicken pieces. Brown all over. Transfer to a large casserole.*

2 *Cook the shallots in the frying pan for 2 minutes. Add to the casserole.*

3 *Add the flour to the frying pan, stir and cook for 2 minutes. Pour in enough wine and stock to make a thin sauce, bring to the boil, stirring all the time, and season to taste.*

4 *Stir in the thyme sprigs, thyme and lavender flowers, orange zest and juice.*

5 ▷ *Pour the sauce over the chicken. Cover the casserole and cook for 30–40 minutes until tender. Remove the thyme sprigs before serving.*

6 *Serve garnished with orange segments and lavender sprigs and flowers.*

LAVENDER JELLY

This is a wonderfully fragrant jelly which captures the essence of summer. It is as versatile as it is lovely and can be served with lamb and smoked chicken or eaten with croissants and scones.

- MAKES 1.8KG/4LB
- INGREDIENTS
  1.8kg/4lb cooking apples,
    washed and chopped
  90ml/6 tbsp lavender flowers
  1.7 litres/3 pint/7½ cups water
  1.36kg/3lb sugar

COOK'S TIP
Lavender often flowers again in September when cooking apples are ripening, so you may prefer to make this in the autumn.

1 *Simmer the apples with 75ml/5 tbsp lavender flowers and water until soft and mushy. Transfer the pulp to a jelly bag and allow the mixture to drip for several hours.*

2 *Measure the resulting liquid and allow 450g/ 1lb sugar to each 600ml/1 pint/2½ cups of liquid. Place the sugar and fruit liquid in a large heavy pan and bring slowly to the boil until setting point is reached. To test, pour 15ml/1 tbsp of the mixture in a saucer and leave to cool. If the top wrinkles when pushed with a finger, the jelly will set.*

3 *Remove from the heat and allow to cool for 20 minutes. Skim off any scum with a slotted spoon.*

4 *Stir in the remaining lavender flowers and pour jelly into small warm sterilized pots (the prettier the better), seal and cover with jam jar covers and rubber bands.*

Casting Nasturtiums

Right: *The nasturtium is one of the best-known and best-loved edible flowers.*

Nasturtiums are marvellous flowers for the garden and kitchen as they are so colourful and tasty. This sun-loving annual comes from Bolivia and Colombia in a range of spectacular colours varying from red and vibrant orange through to pale yellow, in either single, semi-double or double forms. Some grow as climbers, up to 3m/10ft high, and will soon create a wonderful wall of colour if given some support; others are treated as trailing or semi-trailing. *Tropaeolum* 'Peach Melba' is a semi-double form with soft creamy-yellow flowers with an orange-red centre. It is a dwarf variety and is particularly beautiful in a pot.

in the garden

Nasturtiums are all easily grown from seed. Sow either indoors in early to mid-spring, and transplant when all risk of frost has passed or sow outdoors in late spring or early summer so that when the seedlings emerge there is no risk of frost.

Nasturtiums prefer a poor diet. If it is too rich they will put on leaf growth at the expense of flowers. Blackfly can be a problem on the growing tips and beneath the leaves. Watch carefully for infestations. As soon as you see them remove the parts affected or treat them with a horticultural soap. Growing them in partial shade rather than full sun seems to make this less of a problem.

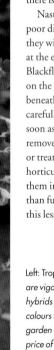

Left: Tropaeolum 'Gleam Series' *are vigorous semi-trailing hybrids with a lovely range of colours that will adapt well to the garden or containers. For the price of a packet of seeds, or just one pot of seedlings, you can create a vibrant focal point in the garden or on the patio.*

Above: *A stone lion wears a fiery mantle made of* Tropaeolum 'Gleam Series'.

GARDENER'S TIP
When planting a chimney pot, find a plastic pot which fits neatly inside. This means you will only have to put compost (soil mix) in the inner liner, and not the entire chimney pot. If the plastic pot is too small, wedge it in place with a piece of wood.

THREE IN ONE

- INGREDIENTS
  - 4 sunflower plants *Helianthus annuus* 'Russian Giant' and 'Velvet Queen'
  - 6 runner (green) bean plants such as *Phaseolus coccineus* 'Scarlet Emperor'
  - 6 climbing nasturtium plants *Tropaeolum majus*
- DRAINAGE Old crocks (china), grit (gravel) or small pieces of polystyrene (plastic foam)
- COMPOST (SOIL MIX) Use fresh compost in containers. Choose either a soil-based compost or a proprietary potting compost (planting mix). This is a thirsty container, packed with plants, so it is advisable to add water-retaining crystals at time of planting
- CONTAINER Large galvanized tub or large wooden half barrel with drainage holes
- PLANT SUPPORTS such as bamboo canes or a willow frame
- SITE Sun or partial shade
- WHEN TO PLANT Early spring as seeds indoors, or late spring outdoors
- AT ITS BEST Mid- to late summer

GARDENER'S TIP
Harvest the runner beans while still young – the more you pick the better the crop. Discard all the contents at the end of the summer. You can save seed from all these plants for the following year.

Choose a very large container such as an old galvanized tub and add a central support structure such as a willow framework or a bundle of bamboo canes tied at the top. Add a generous layer of drainage material and then sow *in situ* (or, if you wish, first in separate pots) sunflowers, runner beans and nasturtiums. By late summer you will have an edible masterpiece.

1 *Cover the base of the container with drainage material. Cover with compost, bringing the level to within 2.5cm/1in of the rim of the container.*

2 *Position the plant supports to create a centre support system.*

3 *Sow the seeds in pairs, with the sunflowers and beans around the base of the supports and the nasturtiums around the edge.*

AFTERCARE
Keep the compost moist at all times. When the seedlings emerge, choose the stronger of each pair and remove the other. As the nasturtiums and beans grow, encourage them to climb up the frame. Some of the nasturtiums may be left to sprawl at the front of the container.

casting nasturtiums

Above: *Nasturtiums provide a sumptuous and generous harvest since not only their flowers but also their leaves, buds and semi-ripe seeds can be eaten.*

Nasturtium flowers are full of colour and have a mild, peppery taste which is excellent in salads. Many flowers have a long spur at their base, and it is here that you will find a drop of sweet nectar that makes them taste particularly good. Choose only the freshest blooms, and eat either whole or just use the petals. They are good cooked in omelettes, added to cream cheese or used as a dressing. Try mixing crushed nasturtium seeds with oil, vinegar, salt and pepper as a vinaigrette for a mixed nasturtium and beetroot (beet) salad. Scatter a few sage flowers on top and you will have a sensationally colourful and tasty supper.

Before you pick the flowers, check that there are no bees hidden among the petals – you could both get a nasty surprise. If tiny pollen beetles are in evidence on the flowers cut the blooms, place the stems in water and cover them with a brown envelope in a dark place (preferably outside) for a while. The beetles will simply fall off and go elsewhere.

NASTURTIUM OMELETTE

This is a spectacularly quick and easy way to serve nasturtium flowers.

- SERVES 1
- INGREDIENTS
  50g/2oz young tender
    runner (green) beans
  2 eggs
  30ml/2 tbsp milk
  2 nasturtium seeds
  2 young nasturtium leaves
  4 nasturtiums, petals only
  salt and ground black pepper
  15ml/1 tbsp butter
  freshly grated parmesan
    cheese, to taste

- TO GARNISH
  nasturtium petals

1 *Slice the runner beans very finely. Add them to a pan of boiling water and boil for 4 minutes. Drain well.*

2 *Beat the eggs with the milk.*

3 △ *Crush the nasturtium seeds with a fork. Add the seeds, leaves and petals to the egg mixture. Season with salt and ground black pepper.*

4 *Melt the butter in a frying pan over a gentle heat.*

5 *Pour the egg and nasturtium mixture into the pan, add the beans and cook gently until the omelette has just set. Sprinkle with parmesan cheese and serve immediately, garnished with extra petals.*

COOK'S TIP
Nasturtium buds and semi-ripe seeds are extremely peppery when eaten raw. Once cooked they lose much of their potency.

A Feast of Fennel

Fennel is a graceful plant that can be grown in different situations. Try containers, herb gardens, among roses, with grasses and sunflowers in a gravel garden or in herbaceous borders. This versatile herb, whether in its green or bronze form, provides a good foil for colourful planting schemes, and will combine beautifully with steely blues, apricots, creams and pinks. Insects love to feed on the flowers in late summer. Fennel will self-seed so remove the numerous seedheads if you wish to avoid lots of seedlings. This is a plant that will tolerate exposed sites.

in the garden

Fennel is a hardy perennial from southern Europe and grows in dry, sunny places. It can reach heights of 1.8m/6ft. It has green or sometimes bronze thread-like leaves with shiny, smooth stems and many heads of tiny bright yellow flowers which cluster together in mid- to late summer. It is easy to grow from seed sown in spring. It is possible to split at the root but this is not always successful as it has a long tap root. Fennel self-seeds readily and although you may not want all the offspring, they can be dug up while still young and transplanted to an appropriate site with success.

in the kitchen

The whole plant can be eaten and tastes of sweet aniseed. Fennel has been eaten for centuries. There is evidence that Roman soldiers ate it for health, while Roman women used it as an appetite suppressant. Fennel was treated much the same as asparagus, with the young stems tied up in bunches, boiled and drained and served with butter and vinegar.

FENNEL SORBET

• SERVES 4

• INGREDIENTS

150g/5oz fresh fennel leaves and stalk

40g/1½oz caster (superfine) sugar

salt and ground black pepper

juice of 1 lemon

fennel flowers, newly opened, with stalks removed

Fennel leaves, flowers and stalk make an unusual sorbet which is a wonderfully cool way to start a meal. This has a low sugar content and so won't be as smooth as traditional sorbets. Do not churn more than 3 hours before serving or it will be too solid.

1 *Wash, drain and finely chop the fennel leaves and stalk. Boil 600ml/1 pint/2½ cups water with a pinch of salt and pepper and caster sugar.*

2 *Add the chopped fennel and boil quickly for 3 minutes. Remove from the heat and allow to infuse for a further 5 minutes, but no longer since the colour will deteriorate.*

3 *Place on ice to cool, and then purée. Strain and adjust the seasoning, then add lemon juice to taste. Add a tablespoon of individual flowers.*

4 *Pour the liquid into an ice tray and freeze until it is just firm around the edges. Beat well, then return the sorbet to the ice tray and freeze until hard. Alternatively use an ice cream maker and churn until firm.*

5 *Scoop the sorbet into 4 chilled glasses and serve immediately, garnished with a sprig of fennel and a scattering of fennel flowers.*

in the kitchen **FENNEL BAGELS WITH SMOKED SALMON**

Fennel leaves, stalks and flowers can be used to make a pretty garnish for freshly baked salmon; here the combination has been adapted to include smoked salmon and this partnership is even more delicious. The smooth cream-cheese filling complements the smoked salmon and is enticingly offset by the aniseed flavour of the tiny yellow flowers.

- SERVES 1
- INGREDIENTS
  1 bagel
  25g/1oz cream cheese
  6–8 small clusters of fennel
    flowers, stalk removed
  1 slice smoked salmon
  a few drops lemon juice
  salt and ground black pepper

1 Cut the bagel in half and spread both halves with a generous covering of cream cheese. Add 2 or 3 yellow flower clusters.

2 Cover the base bagel half with a slice of salmon, sprinkle with lemon juice and season to taste.

3 Add the top bagel half and serve decorated with a few more flowers along the front and sides.

COOK'S TIP

If a whole bagel seems too thick, serve the halves open-faced. Fennel leaves can be added for additional colour and flavour. They soon wilt when cut from the plant so snip them very small.

Cottage Classic

Right: The rich colours of hollyhock flowers enhance the garden and kitchen.

Hollyhocks are natives of temperate regions in Europe and Asia, usually growing on rocky outcrops and dry grassy areas. In the garden they rise up like tall cathedral spires, 1.5–2.5m/5–8ft high, producing delicate papery flowers in succession for many weeks throughout the summer. They can be found as a single flower or as doubles, in a wide range of colours ranging from white to pale yellow, pink, mauve and deep, rich purple.

Their large flowers offer generous pollen supplies and on warm summer days, lazy bees can be seen searching from flower to flower for their daily sup.

in the garden

Grow hollyhocks at the back of a border where they will add height and elegance, or plant them in front of a climbing rose where you can look through their giant flower stems to see the roses behind.

In a cottage garden, hollyhocks can grow almost anywhere they like, either the front or back of the border, or beside a path, gate or steps. They will look at home wherever they are. What is more, bees are sure to find them.

Hollyhocks will self-seed with ease, growing in the most surprising places, and before long you will have a whole range of colours. Modern hybrids can be sown in spring to flower later that same summer, while most seedlings will only produce flowers the second year.

Unfortunately, rust affects the leaves and causes unsightly disfigurement. Remove those afflicted. The flowers will still look pretty but you are probably best discarding the plants at the end of the summer.

Left: If possible, choose a sunny and sheltered site for hollyhocks. They will grow so tall that they require supports to prevent wind damage. Stake them individually or tie in with string. A bushy, dwarf variety, such as 'Majorette', grows only 1m/3ft high and so is less susceptible to breakage.

WARNING

The flowers are full of pollen, which may cause problems for hay-fever sufferers. If using in the kitchen, remove the central reproductive organs, trim off the green calyx and dust off all the pollen.

in the kitchen

Above: *To prepare hollyhock petals,
remove the stigma from the centre of
the hollyhock, cut off the green parts
and you will have five petals
remaining. Brush off any excess
pollen from the petals.*

Hollyhocks are members of the mallow family which were one of the most common pot and salad herbs throughout the Middle Ages. Earlier still, mallow farming was greatly valued by the Romans, Egyptians and Chinese. For medicinal and culinary purposes, the marsh mallow was regarded as the most important of all herbs. It was used to make both syrups and pickles, and in the early spring the tender mallow stalks were preserved in sugar. The flowers were used with other ingredients as a gargle.

Hollyhock flowers can be used in the same way, and although they do not have a strong flavour, their texture is pleasant, and their beauty unquestionable. A wide range of colours is available so you can mix and match different fruit and flowers to best effect.

in the kitchen

HOLLYHOCK AND NECTARINE SALAD

The fresh, juicy flavour and beautiful colouring of nectarines lend themselves to an arrangement with hollyhock petals. Choose your hollyhock petals to contrast or blend with the fruit. Watermelon would make an equally cheerful partner.

- SERVES 2
- INGREDIENTS
  2 nectarines, either white or
    yellow flesh
  2 hollyhock flowers
  2 sprigs flowering ginger mint

1 *Cut the nectarines in half, remove the stones (pits) and slice the fruit. Arrange the slices on individual serving plates.*

2 *Remove the stigma from the centre of the hollyhocks, then cut off all the green parts. Brush any excess pollen off the petals.*

3 *Arrange the petals around the nectarine slices and garnish with the mint flowers.*

COOK'S TIP
A mint flower syrup could be poured over the fruit. Use 300ml/
½ pint/1¼ cups of water to 450g/1lb caster (superfine) or
granulated (white) sugar. Dissolve the sugar in the water, add
6 sprigs of mint flowers and then bring to the boil until the
mixture turns into a syrup. Cool, strain and bottle, and keep in
the refrigerator for up to 2 weeks.

Some Enchanted Evening

Right: The pale yellow colouring of the evening primrose is one of the joys of late summer.

Evening primrose is a plant which has an unusual flowering pattern. The very pretty yellow petals only open in the evening, perfuming the air with their sweet fragrance. The flowers then stay out during the night, and close towards lunch time. Although each flower is short-lived there is a long succession of blooms, so for many weeks you will have plenty of flowers to pick and enjoy in the kitchen.

The seeds of the plant are used to make evening primrose oil which is often sold to alleviate pre-menstrual tension, menopausal complaints and many other problems.

in the garden

Evening primrose is a native of eastern North America and likes plenty of sun on a dry, stony site. It grows 1–1.5m/3–5ft tall with a spread of at least 60cm/24in – often more if it does not remain upright. Because of its height, it is best planted where it has plenty of room to flaunt its flowers. It is ideal in a sunny sheltered corner of a building where you can enjoy its scent.

Evening primrose is easily grown from seed sown *in situ* in the autumn, or in pots in early summer. It is a prolific self-seeder. During its first year you will see a rosette of tapering leaves. The second summer you will have a large flowering plant.

Left: The evening primrose begins to flower in mid-summer and continues right through to the autumn.

GARDENER'S TIP

If too many plants self-seed in the garden, you can dig up a few and boil the roots, which taste like sweet parsnip. The leaf and stem were once a favourite food of some Native American tribes.

in the kitchen

*Right: Evening primrose
petals can be used as a
simple garnish to enhance
many fruits, including all
types of melon.*

E̲ach evening primrose flower has a long tube and four petals. Like day lilies, both the bud and the flower can be eaten. The young leaves, stalks and roots are also edible. The flavour of evening primrose is very fresh, with a hint of sweetness similar to its scent. It is a welcome addition to any late summer salad, whether it is a savoury green or a fruit-based salad. Combine the pale yellow flowers with delicately coloured fruit.

in the kitchen

LUNCHTIME SALAD OF EVENING PRIMROSE PETALS

The pretty yellow petals of the evening primrose make a delightful addition to this light, crunchy salad – a meal in itself with plenty of visual appeal. This salad could be prepared with 60ml/4 tbsp crème fraîche, plain (natural) yogurt or thick mayonnaise instead of the cottage cheese, if you prefer a creamier texture. Prosciutto might also be added. This recipe could easily be adapted for a finger buffet by filling chicory (Belgian endive) cavities with the cottage cheese mixture.

• SERVES 4–6
• INGREDIENTS
  2 red dessert apples
  juice of ½ lemon
  250g/8oz cottage cheese
  50g/2oz sunflower seeds

4 heads Little Gem (Bibb)
  lettuce
4 pineapple rings, halved
6 evening primrose buds
petals from 10 evening
  primrose flowers

1 *Slice the apples into a bowl and pour the lemon juice over them.*

2 *Mix the cottage cheese with the sunflower seeds and arrange in the centre of a large platter with a circle of apple slices on top.*

3 *Prepare the little gem lettuces and use the leaves to create a circle of greenery around the cottage cheese mixture. Place the pineapple pieces in between the lettuce leaves.*

4 *Remove all the green parts from the evening primrose flowers and buds. Scatter the buds and petals over the salad and serve.*

COOK'S TIP
These flowers are daylight sensitive. They will be open for a very late supper and will still be open for lunch the following day but not for early evening. The buds are available at any time. If you cut the flower spikes ready to use in the kitchen, be sure to put the vase by a sunny window as they soon close when out of the sun.

Flowering Courgette

Right: 'Burpee Golden Zucchini' produces masses of golden flowers. They should be harvested frequently to ensure a continuous supply.

When growing courgettes (zucchini) in the garden, there are several different varieties to choose from. The one illustrated here is Courgette 'Burpee Golden Zucchini' which is a fine cropper producing a wonderful harvest of succulent yellow fruit. Sometimes the foliage of this variety has yellow blotches on the leaves while it is still young. This is nothing to worry about, and indeed it can look attractive in the garden set against other foliage.

In France and Italy the flowers are often sold in the marketplace. As this is less common in other countries it is best to grow them in the garden.

in the garden

Courgettes may be sown in two ways. If you want an earlier crop, sow the seeds indoors in spring, harden young plants off by putting them outside in the daytime, then towards the end of spring or early summer, when all risk of frost has passed, transplant outside, positioned 1m/3ft apart in a sunny spot in the garden. Or, sow in pairs directly into prepared ground in the garden, 2.5cm/1in deep, where they are to grow and fruit. Thin to the strongest seedling. Protect young plants if frost threatens. Grow five to eight plants to produce a good harvest of flowers. They also grow well in medium to large containers.

Keep soil moist at all times and once they have started flowering apply a liquid feed once a week. Cut either the male or female flowers for use as edible flowers (though out of preference only take the male ones) and harvest the young courgettes regularly to encourage further production when they are about 10–15cm/4–6in long.

Right: Courgettes produce separate male and female flowers. Both are edible, but if you harvest the female flowers you will arrest the formation of fruit. So where possible, choose the male flowers. The difference is immediately obvious. The female flower already has the embryo fruit behind the petals while the male flower just has the stem. Inside the flower, the female ovary is very swollen.

GARDENER'S TIP

When picking courgette flowers beware of large, feasting bees. Also look out for tiny rape or pollen beetles which are attracted to the centre of the yellow flowers. They can be removed by placing the flowers in a darkened environment, preferably outside, where they will soon drop off. Alternatively, brush them off as you remove the petals or flood the flowers with water before you use them.

in the kitchen

Right: The courgette harvest produces a double crop, both of flowers and fruit.

Courgette flowers can be eaten hot or cold. They have a fine, mellow flavour which makes them a popular flower for many food recipes. In Mediterranean countries they are often stuffed with rice or cheese fillings, or they are coated in a pancake-type batter and cooked as fritters. Their history as a culinary flower is a long one; native Americans ate squash flowers long before the arrival of the Spanish to North America.

in the kitchen

TAGLIATELLE WITH COURGETTE FLOWERS

This recipe uses only the courgette petals, rather than the whole flower. Their silky texture lends itself well to that of tagliatelle, while the flavour of the bacon and chives is wholly complementary. Often, as the flowers are produced, baby courgettes are busy forming on the same plants. This recipe makes the most of the baby courgette's sweet flavour, resulting in a delicious pasta dish.

• SERVES 4

• INGREDIENTS

18 courgette (zucchini) flowers
50g/2oz butter
½ onion, chopped
115g/4oz Parma ham or unsmoked bacon, diced
4 baby courgettes (zucchini), thinly sliced

15ml/1 tbsp chopped chives
salt and ground black pepper
350g/12oz dried egg tagliatelle
115g/4oz freshly grated Parmesan cheese

1 *Using a sharp knife, slit down one side of the courgette flowers. Remove the stalks and stamens and discard. Wipe the prepared flowers carefully and cut into strips.*

2 *In a large pan, heat the butter and sauté the onion and ham over a low heat for about 5 minutes.*

3 *Add the sliced courgettes and chives and cook for a further 2 minutes. Season and reduce the heat so that the mixture is kept just warm.*

4 *Cook the tagliatelle in plenty of boiling water until al dente. Drain.*

5 *Add the courgette flowers to the sauce, cook for just a minute, then toss in the tagliatelle. Add the Parmesan cheese and serve immediately.*

Bergamot Infusion

Above: Each flower is rich in colour and full of flavour.

Bergamot is a hardy perennial from eastern North America which was introduced to England by Peter Collinson in 1744. It can be grown in massed clumps in an herbaceous border, or in smaller clumps in the herb garden. It looks equally in keeping in a cottage garden or in large containers.

The species *Monarda didyma* has pink or scarlet flowers. Several improved colours are available as garden plants. 'Cambridge Scarlet' has rich scarlet red flowers, 'Beauty of Cobham' has pink and pale purple flowers, while 'Croftway Pink' has rose-pink colouring. *Monarda fistula,* known as wild bergamot, is a close relative which is slightly taller than the others and grows about 1.2m/4ft tall. It has pink or mauve flowers, which have a very strong flavour.

in the garden   HERBAL TEA BARREL

This container is rich with the fragrance of eau de cologne, peppermint and lemon. All the leaves can be infused to make teas, but it is the bergamot that is the star. Its brilliant red flowers protrude in large whorls, each long, tubular flower packed with sweetness.

- INGREDIENTS
  1 bergamot plant *Monarda* 'Cambridge Scarlet'
  1 golden lemon balm plant *Melissa officinalis* 'Aurea'
  1 peppermint plant *Mentha x piperata*
  1 eau de cologne mint plant *Mentha x piperata f. citrata*

- PLANT SUPPORTS Such as metal plant rings, twigs or shortened bamboo canes and garden string
- DRAINAGE Old crocks (china), grit (gravel) or small pieces of polystyrene (plastic foam)
- COMPOST (SOIL MIX) Use fresh compost in containers. Choose either a soil-based compost or a proprietary potting compost (planting

mix). This is a thirsty container packed with plants so it is advisable to add a water-retaining gel
- CONTAINER Large wooden half barrel with drainage holes
- SITE Sun or light shade
- WHEN TO PLANT Spring
- AT ITS BEST Mid- to late summer

1 *Cover the base of the container with a generous layer of drainage material. Cover with compost bringing the level to within 2.5cm/1in of the rim of the container.*

2 *Plant the bergamot at the centre back with the lemon balm centre front and the two mints on either side.*

3 *Water well and firm in the plants.*

AFTERCARE
Keep the compost moist at all times. Provide supports once the bergamot has reached 60cm/24in. Cut down all growth in late autumn to within 10cm/4in of soil level. Add a fine layer of new compost in the spring and apply a general fertilizer.

in the kitchen

Right: The long tubular flowers of the bergamot are easily removed from the head – simply pull them away. The white end is very sweet tasting.

Bergamot was a favourite drink of the Oswegan Indians of North America and it became a popular tea substitute in New England after the Boston Tea Party of 1773. The flower and leaves can be used on their own or added to Earl Grey tea leaves to create a refreshing drink. The flowers are exceptionally beautiful and packed full of sweet flavour. They can be used fresh, scattered on salads, added to pasta, or eaten in rice dishes. To enjoy the flowers out of season, preserve them in oil or vinegar.

in the kitchen

BERGAMOT RICE SALAD

The beautiful red bergamot flowers make a striking contrast to the glistening black olives, juicy mushrooms and grains of wild rice. Serve with fresh mackerel or white fish.

- SERVES 4–6 PEOPLE
- INGREDIENTS

250g/8oz wild rice or mixed rice with wild rice grains
125g/8oz flat mushrooms, thickly sliced
30ml/2 tbsp olive oil
4 young bergamot leaves, thinly shredded
115g/4oz black olives
salt and ground black pepper
15–30ml/1–2 tbsp of pink or red bergamot petals

1 *Simmer the rice in a pan of boiling water for 25–30 minutes until soft, then drain.*

2 *Place the sliced mushrooms in a frying pan with the olive oil and cook gently for 4 minutes.*

3 *Add the bergamot leaves and olives and mix together. Season to taste with salt and ground black pepper.*

4 *Add the cooked wild rice to the mushrooms and other ingredients and toss together. Lastly mix in the bergamot petals.*

Look to the Sun

Above: Be sure to stake very tall sunflowers otherwise strong winds may snap the stem.

Sunflowers are native to North America, where they grow as tall annuals. Selected hybrids such as 'Russian Giant' can sometimes reach 4.5m/15ft. Sunflowers enjoy sunny, sheltered spots, and can be grown in deep containers or in the garden. Dwarf varieties are now easily available such as 'Pacino', 30cm/12in and 'Sunspot', 60cm/24in. They are ideal for window-boxes or pots. Although most sunflowers are bright yellow, there are colour variations. 'Velvet Queen' is rich mahogany-red with bronze tips and 'Lemon Queen' is much lighter in colouring.

Sunflowers are easy to grow from seed and can be sown indoors in early or mid-spring 1cm/½in deep, or outdoors in late spring when they can be planted 2.5cm/1in directly in the ground or in the container where they are to mature. The earlier the sowing the sooner they will flower.

in the garden A FEAST OF FLOWERS IN A WINDOW-BOX

Although a large window-box has been used here, this scheme would adapt very easily to any large pot.

- INGREDIENTS
  12 sunflower seeds
  Helianthus annuus
  'Sunspot'
  12 nasturtium seeds
  Tropaeolum majus 'Double
  Gleam Mixed'

- DRAINAGE Old crocks (china), grit (gravel) or small pieces of polystyrene (plastic foam)
- COMPOST (SOIL MIX) Use fresh compost in containers. Choose either a soil-based compost or a proprietary potting compost (planting mix). This is a thirsty container, packed with plants, so it is advisable to add water-retaining

crystals at the time of planting
- CONTAINER Large window-box 80cm/32in long, 20cm/8in wide, 17.5cm/7in deep
- SITE Sunny
- WHEN TO PLANT Early spring as seeds indoors, or late spring outdoors
- AT ITS BEST Mid- to late summer

1 *Cover the base of the container with 2.5cm/1in drainage material. Add compost bringing level to within 2.5cm/1in of the rim of the container. Water the compost well.*

2 ▷ *Sow 6 pairs of sunflower seeds at the back and 6 pairs of nasturtium seeds at the front, at a depth of around 1–2.5cm/½–1in. After germination, remove the weaker seedling of each pair.*

in the kitchen

Right: *Sunflower 'Velvet Queen'
produces a wealth of small
flowers over a very long period.*

Sunflower petals are an excellent addition to salads. The petals have a mild, nutty taste and add colour and flavour to breads and pasta. The buds can be eaten too, although they need blanching to remove any bitterness. Once blanched, drain and steam or boil for another three minutes. Toss them in garlic butter and enjoy the flavour akin to their cousin the Jerusalem artichoke. The kernel inside the seed is rich in Vitamin B1, B2, niacin, iron, phosphorous, vegetable fats and protein.

in the kitchen ## PETAL AND SEED BREAD

Sunflower seeds are frequently added to breads and rolls. Here, the petals are included as well. To make an interesting coloured loaf you can add a few strands of saffron.

- MAKES ONE 500G/
  1LB 2OZ LOAF
- INGREDIENTS
  ½ sachet (envelope) saffron
  (optional)
  50g/2oz sunflower seeds
  280g/10oz packet of white
  bread mix

15ml/1tbsp mustard seeds or
onion seeds
5ml/1tsp curry powder
petals of 1 sunflower
salt and ground black pepper
milk, to glaze

1 *If using, put the saffron in a small bowl with 30ml/2 tbsp boiling water and leave for 5 minutes. Heat the sunflower seeds in a frying pan for 3–4 minutes until just beginning to colour. Leave to cool.*

2 *Put the bread mix in a bowl with the saffron and liquid, and add all but 30ml/2tbsp of the sunflower seeds, the mustard or onion seeds, curry powder and a little seasoning. Pull the petals from the sunflower and add to the bowl. Add 175ml/6fl oz of hand-hot water and mix to a dough. Turn out on to a floured surface and knead gently for 5 minutes.*

3 *Place in a lightly oiled 500g/1lb 2oz loaf tin (pan) and cover loosely with oiled cling film (plastic wrap). Leave in a warm place until the dough has risen well above the top of the tin. Preheat the oven to 220ºC/425ºF/Gas 7.*

4 *Brush the top of the loaf lightly with milk. Score the bread diagonally several times and sprinkle with the remaining sunflower seeds. Bake for 15 minutes until turning golden, then reduce the oven temperature to 180ºC/350ºF/Gas 4 and bake for a further 15 minutes. Turn out of the tin and leave to cool on a wire rack.*

COOK'S TIP
A simple method of making sunflower baguettes is to buy ready-prepared dough and place the sunflower petals over the surface of the dough before rolling up and placing in the oven. The flavouring from the petals is scrumptiously nutty.

Aromatic Basil

Right: *Basil may be purchased as a punnet of seedlings from the supermarket. They soon grow on to produce many fine plants.*

Basil is an aromatic herb from Africa and Asia packed with warmth and flavour to match. It will grow 30–60cm/2–3ft high. Several varieties are available, one of the commonest being the broad-leaved green basil which has white flowers. But there are also purple-leaved kinds such as 'Purple Ruffles' and 'Dark Opal' with small but lovely mauve purple flowers, as well as cinnamon- and lemon-flavoured types.

Seed sown in spring needs 13°C/55°F heat to germinate, and thereafter should be kept in the warmth of a greenhouse or window-sill indoors until summer days lengthen. It can be sown directly outside in summer.

in the garden TOMATO AND BASIL TOWER

Basil and tomatoes go hand in hand in the kitchen so why not plant a tomato and basil tower to provide summer flavours? The choice of tomatoes may vary considerably, but the ones grown here are 'Gardener's Delight'. This is a companion planting scheme using basil to ward off any white fly from the tomatoes.

- INGREDIENTS
  3 tomato plants *Tomato* 'Gardener's Delight'
  3 basil plants or clumps of seedlings *Ocimum basilicum*

- PLANT SUPPORTS Use a willow or metal framework, or simply create a wigwam (teepee) of bamboo canes tied together at the top

- DRAINAGE Old crocks (china), grit (gravel) or small pieces of polystyrene (plastic foam)
- COMPOST (SOIL MIX) Choose either a soil-based compost or a proprietary potting compost (planting mix). Add water-retaining crystals to the compost at the time of planting
- CONTAINER Large pot or half barrel, 30cm/1ft deep by

60cm/2ft across
- SITE In a greenhouse until mid-summer, then move outside to a sunny sheltered spot, if preferred
- WHEN TO PLANT Early summer
- AT ITS BEST Mid-summer to autumn

1 *Cover the base of the container with 5cm/2in of drainage material and add enough compost to bring level to within 2.5cm/1in of the rim.*

2 *If you are using a fixed frame put this in place.*

3 ◁ *Alternate the three tomato plants with the basil in a wide circle near the edge of the container.*

4 *Water well. Firm in the plants and put the plant support system in place if you have not already done so.*

in the kitchen

Right: *Basil flowers are produced freely in late summer just when the tomatoes ripen.*

B asil flowers may be small but they certainly have a beautifully aromatic flavour and are surprisingly sweet. They can be used fresh in all sorts of ways by adding them with basil leaves to tomato salads or pizza toppings, scattered on pastas, or used as flavourings in tomato juice. To remove the flowers from the stem, simply pull – they will come away easily. Purple-leaved basil has a pretty mauve flower which is delicious too.

in the kitchen

CHILLED TOMATO AND BASIL-FLOWER SOUP

This is a really fresh tasting soup, packed with the complementary flavours of tomato and basil and topped with sweet basil flowers.

- SERVES 4
- INGREDIENTS
  900g/2lb tomatoes
  1 onion
  1 clove garlic, crushed
  15ml/1 tbsp olive oil
  600ml/1 pint/2½ cups

  vegetable stock
  20 basil leaves
  a few drops of elderflower or
    balsamic vinegar
  juice of ½ lemon
  150ml/¼ pint/⅔ cup plain
    (natural) yogurt

  sugar and salt, to taste

- TO GARNISH
  10ml/2 tsp basil flowers, all
    green parts removed
  8 small basil leaves
  30ml/2 tbsp plain yogurt

1 *Chop the tomatoes roughly, then peel and chop the onion and garlic.*

2 *Fry the onion and garlic in the oil for 2–3 minutes until soft and transparent.*

3 *Add 300ml/½ pint/1¼ cups stock to the pan, then add the tomatoes.*

4 *Bring to the boil, then lower the heat and simmer for 15 minutes.*

5 *Allow to cool slightly, liquidize and strain to remove the tomato skins and seeds.*

6 *Add the remainder of the stock, half the basil leaves, vinegar, lemon juice and yogurt to the tomato purée. Season with sugar and salt to taste. Process until smooth. Chill.*

7 *Just before serving finely shred the remaining basil leaves and add to the soup.*

8 *Pour the chilled soup into individual bowls. Garnish with yogurt topped with a few small basil leaves and a scattering of basil flowers on each serving.*

Menthol Magic

Above: Mentha spicota *produces*
tall spikes of blue flowers
in late summer.

Mint is probably one of our most familiar garden herbs. *Mentha suaveolens* has rounded foliage and is an excellent culinary variety with a sweet apple-mint taste. Its variegated form *M.s.* 'Variegata' is more ornamental but still has a very good flavour. *M. spicata* tastes of spearmint. Try different varieties for different flavours: *M.* x *piperata* has a strong peppermint aroma and taste while its close relative, *M.* x *piperata f. citrata,* has justly celebrated, delightfully perfumed leaves, scented just like eau de cologne. *M. gracilis*, known as ginger mint, is perhaps less well known but a good variegated variety with a warm, spicy flavour. These all grow between 40cm–90cm/16–36in high. There are many others besides. All have small edible mauve flowers, but with their unique scents they can be used in a wide variety of ways.

in the garden

All varieties of mint can be grown outside in the garden, although being rather vigorous in habit they might soon swamp smaller, less intrusive plants. If you are worried, plant them in the garden in a bottomless deep bucket or plastic pot with the bottom half buried in soil to prevent

unwanted colonization. You will still have to keep an eye on the plants as the peppermint and eau de cologne varieties send out surface runners. Mint likes a sunny or partially sunny spot with moisture. Divide plants every three years to regenerate the rootstock, otherwise the flavour might deteriorate.

Propagation is very easy as all small roots, even with one growing node, will create a new plant if planted in good compost (soil mix) or left in the garden soil. Alternatively, take tip-cuttings and insert in a bottle or water. Take care to keep the water level high so that the roots remain immersed. Within just a matter of days, roots will grow and the cuttings can then be potted up.

Mints can also be grown in containers. Trap them at the bottom of a herb hanging basket where they can't escape and where they can give a generous cloak to the sides of the basket. *M.s.* 'Variegata' has beautifully soft variegated foliage which always looks good with other plants. *M.* x *piperata f. citrata* is also recommended, as it will release its strong but lovely eau de cologne scent whenever it is touched or watered. By mid-to late summer, metallic purple runners from the eau de cologne mint shoot out from the sides of baskets seeking new ground in which to root. Hanging in mid-air their mission is hopeless; not so on the ground!

Left: *Mint grows exuberantly in the*
garden. It makes a lush addition to a
hanging basket.

GARDENER'S TIP

If brown rust spores appear on the leaves, remove the plants in the garden and burn them. If it happens to container plants, cut the stems right down to soil level and destroy later.

in the kitchen

Mint leaves and flowers can be used in a variety of ways in the kitchen: add to new potatoes and other vegetables, sauces and drinks. Eau de cologne mint and lemon verbena can be used in tandem to make refreshing teas. Another lovely summery idea is to pour boiling water over eau de cologne mint leaves and flowers, strain the liquid and use to flavour an orange jelly. Ginger mint flowers work well with fruit salads, or blend cucumber, yogurt and mint leaves and flowers to make a delicious chilled soup. Mint flower and crab-apple jelly is another tasty idea, wonderful with lamb or simply bread and cheese.

Left: *Variegated mint makes a flavoursome and attractive addition to many summer drinks.*

in the kitchen

MINT-FLOWER VINEGAR

This makes an excellent vinegar for salad dressings, and can be used in a classic vinaigrette dressing. The mint flavour will be particularly appreciated in winter when the fresh leaves are unavailable.

• MAKES 450ML/¾ PINT/
2 CUPS

• INGREDIENTS
120ml/8 tbsp mint flowers
with stems and leaves
attached
450ml/¾ pint/2 cups white
wine vinegar

WARNING
Avoid aluminium pans because the acid will react with the aluminium. Use a glass or steel pan or heat in a glass jug (pitcher) in the microwave.

1 Place the mint flowers in a jar with a non-metallic lid. A kilner jar is ideal.

2 Heat the vinegar gently but do not allow it to boil.

3 ▷ Pour the heated vinegar over the flowers, bringing the level to within 1.5cm/½in of the rim of the jar.

4 Allow the mixture to cool before putting the lid on.

5 Leave for 3–4 weeks, then strain and pour into a clean jar or a recycled vinegar bottle.

6 ▷ Add fresh mint flowers for decoration and label the jar or bottle.

Rich Hyssop

Hyssop is native to southern Europe where it grows as a low shrubby plant 60cm/2ft high, producing long slender stems crammed with bright blue flowers from mid-summer to early autumn. White, pink and purple forms are also available.

In the past hyssop was often grown as an edge to formal flower beds, where it was kept tightly clipped each spring.

Left: Hyssop produces dense flower spikes from mid-summer to early autumn.

in the garden

Hyssop likes a light sandy or alkaline soil and will grow in sun or partial shade. Plant it among alpine pinks and violas in a herb bed or cottage garden, or grow it beneath a standard or weeping rose where it can be used as a general underplanting or, more formally clipped, to provide a low hedge. It is excellent in containers including summer hanging baskets. Bees and butterflies are attracted to its flowers.

Right: Hyssop combines beautifully with many smaller plants such as violas, alpine pinks and thymes. Viola 'Rebecca' makes the perfect partner with its creamy face and mauve-blue fringe.

Propagate by seeds sown in early spring or autumn or by stem cuttings taken in early summer. Cut back after flowering in mild areas or, in spring where winters are harsher, to within 20cm/8in of the ground, to remove straggly growth and promote a good shape for the following year.

in the kitchen

The flower spike grows in long wands, producing blooms at the bottom first, slowly working up the stem. Meanwhile the top of the stem is formed of tightly closed buds. In the past, the tops and flowers were used in soups and tossed on salads. Hyssop tea was made by adding boiling water to the green flower buds. The flowers can also be used to make hyssop vinegar, oil and butter. Although the flowers are small they have a strong flavour that resembles a combination of thyme and menthol. Newly opened flowers are sweet at the base.

in the kitchen CHICKEN-LIVER PATE WITH HYSSOP

This is a deliciously rich-flavoured pâté which can be served with toast or crusty bread. Make a simple tomato or green salad garnished with extra hyssop flowers to accompany the pâté.

- SERVES 6–8
- INGREDIENTS

50g/2oz butter
115g/4oz bacon, chopped
2 cloves garlic crushed
1 small onion, finely chopped
450g/1lb chicken livers, chopped
salt and ground black pepper
60ml/4 tbsp hyssop flowers and tops, stems removed
60ml/4 tbsp dry sherry
60ml/4 tbsp double (heavy) cream
5ml/1 tsp lemon juice

- TO GARNISH

75g/3oz melted butter
1–2 sprigs of hyssop flowers and tops

1 *Melt the butter in a pan, add the bacon, garlic and onion and cook gently for 4 minutes.*

2 *Stir in the chicken livers and cook for a further 5 minutes.*

3 *Add the salt, pepper, hyssop flowers and tops, and sherry and cook until the liquid has evaporated.*

4 *Leave to cool, then blend in a liquidizer with the cream and lemon juice.*

5 *Empty the contents into a pâté dish and top with melted butter. Place in a refrigerator overnight to set.*

6 *Complete the garnish with sprigs of hyssop in flower.*

COOK'S TIP
This is an excellent pâté to freeze and enjoy at a later date. Simply place in an airtight container and label.

Mediterranean Marjoram

Many different marjorams are available but they will all enjoy dry sunny conditions. The leaves are especially aromatic, and the flowers taste like a sweeter version of the foliage. They are a favourite of bees and butterflies and can be grown beside a sunny path in a cottage garden, or among other herbs and roses in a herb garden. The golden-leaved or gold-tipped ones look particularly pleasing.

Marjoram can be divided easily in spring and can also be grown from seed. It is excellent in pots where it will bask in the warmth of the terracotta. Marjoram is also a welcome addition to a spring or summer flowering basket. Cut the stems back to ground level in the autumn or early spring.

Above: Marjoram flowers form in dense clusters from mid-summer to early autumn.

in the garden   STRAWBERRY AND MARJORAM POT

In this pot, strawberries and later flowering marjoram have been combined to give a long season of interest and a welcome harvest of fruit and flowers in both mid- and late summer. *Origanum vulgare*, a reliable and prolific flowerer, was planted with the pretty foliage of 'Country Cream' and 'Aureum Crispum'. The variegated lemon balm adds height to the centre of the pot and has tiny white edible flowers in mid- to late summer.

- INGREDIENTS
  1 marjoram plant *Origanum vulgare*
  1 marjoram plant *Origanum vulgare* 'Aureum Crispum'
  1 marjoram plant *Origanum vulgare* 'Country Cream'
  1 variegated golden lemon balm plant *Melissa officinalis* 'Aurea'
  6 strawberry plants *Fragaria x ananassa* 'Calypso' or 'Cambridge Favourite'

- DRAINAGE Old crocks (china), grit (gravel) or small pieces of polystyrene (plastic foam)
- COMPOST (SOIL MIX) Use fresh compost in containers. Choose either a soil-based compost or a proprietary potting compost (planting mix). This pot will dry out quickly so it is advisable to add water-retaining crystals at the time of planting

- CONTAINER This type of pot is called either a herb pot, a parsley pot or a strawberry pot. It was particularly good for planting as it had six large holes around the sides. Avoid ones with small openings. This one is 25cm/10in diameter and 23cm/9in deep
- SITE Sunny
- WHEN TO PLANT Early spring
- AT ITS BEST Mid-summer to autumn

Left: The strawberry chosen here is 'Calypso,' a recent variety with good, firm, shiny fruit which ripen in early summer and has another crop later in the season. 'Cambridge Favourite' would be another good choice and is widely available. If you want a strawberry with the flavour and aroma of a wild strawberry but the size of a cultivated strawberry then choose 'Mara des Bois'.

in the garden

1 *Cover the base of the container with 2.5cm/1in of drainage material and add enough compost to bring it level with the bottom of the lowest hole.*

2 △ *Alternate three strawberry plants and three marjorams through the holes around the sides of the pot. Here the strawberries were planted in the higher tier. Add more compost, making sure that each root is embedded securely.*

Above: Origanum vulgare *'Country Cream'* is very pretty but it needs protection from full sun.

3 △ *Plant the remaining strawberries round the edge in the top of the pot, arranging them so that they are not directly above the strawberry plants below. Plant the lemon balm in the centre.*

4 *Fill in any gaps with compost, bringing the compost level to within 2.5cm/1in from the top of the container. Water well. Firm in the plants and add more compost if necessary.*

AFTERCARE

Keep the compost moist at all times. 'Country Cream' is liable to scorch marks around the edges of its leaves if the sun is too strong. Either remove offending leaves (new ones will soon grow) or make sure that the plant is on the shadier side of the pot. Crop the strawberries as they ripen and enjoy snippets of the marjoram and lemon balm throughout the growing season. Cut down growth on the lemon balm to within 8cm/3in of the soil level at least once during early summer in order to contain the growth and renew the lovely foliage. Cut all the marjorams back to within 5cm/2in of the base after flowering to encourage new growth. Apply a liquid feed every week once the strawberries have started forming fruit. Enjoy the late strawberry crop as well as the early crop and pick the marjoram flowers when newly opened. All these plants will last over the winter, but for a repeat scheme for the following year, empty the pot in early spring and replant using fresh compost. Divide the marjorams and lemon balm and plant the excess elsewhere in the garden. The straw-berries may be less easy to separate and it might be better to start again.

Above: *Strawberry flowers are produced in early summer and again in late summer.*

Above: Marjoram flowers can
be infused to make herbal tea or
preserved to flavour oils,
vinegar and butter.

M arjoram leaves have a strongly aromatic flavour varying slightly depending on which varieties you choose. The actual flowers – sweeter than the leaves – are tiny but numerous, growing in large clusters. Either remove them individually, or for a stronger flavour cut the stems and harvest the green calyx and petals intact. Always choose newly opened flower heads as these have the greatest flavour and are the most tender.

The flowers can be used to flavour many chicken and fish dishes, may be added to stuffings, salads and pasta, as well as many sauces. They are lovely in a cheese quiche, or mixed with breadcrumbs and olive oil and scattered on top of roasted vegetables.

in the kitchen CIABATTA BREAD WITH MARJORAM FLOWERS

- SERVES 2
- INGREDIENTS
  1 ciabatta loaf
  4 medium tomatoes
  115g/4oz mozzarella or
    Cheddar cheese
  15ml/1 tbsp olive oil
  salt and ground black pepper
  15ml/1 tbsp marjoram
    flowers

Here is a very simple but tasty method of using marjoram flowers. The combination of cheese, tomato and marjoram is popular, but lots of extras can be added such as capers, olives, anchovies or roasted (bell) peppers.

1 Cut the loaf in half lengthways and toast very lightly under the grill (broiler) until it has turned a pale golden brown.

2 Meanwhile skin the tomatoes. Slash the bottoms and tops and pour boiling water over until the skin begins to recede. Drain off the water and allow to cool before removing the skin and cutting into thick slices.

3 Slice or grate the cheese. Lightly drizzle oil over the bread and cover with the cheese and tomato slices. Add the seasoning and scatter the marjoram flowers over the top. Drizzle with a little more olive oil. Return to the grill until the cheese melts.

COOK'S TIP
Add the flowers to your favourite pizza topping. Scatter over 7.5–15ml/ ½–1 tbsp flowers or flowering tops and add a few of the leaves. The flavours are strong so the amount you use will depend on your own palate.

sowing seeds

indoors outdoors

combination planting

self-seeding plants

taking cuttings

Propagating Techniques

Most of the edible flowers mentioned in this book are easily

found for sale in garden centres and nurseries as plants or seeds.

Where they are already growing as plants it is easy to buy them

and transfer them into containers or straight into the garden.

However, it is much cheaper and certainly much more fun to

propagate your own.

Right: *Many edible flowers can be propagated
at home in the potting shed.*

Sowing Seeds

Growing plants from seed is an inexpensive and easy way to raise edible flowers. Seeds for courgettes (zucchini) will cost only a few pennies per plant so an entire crop will cost less than the cost of one courgette in the supermarket. You will be able to gather courgette flowers for many weeks and have the courgettes as a bonus.

Annual plants that can be grown from seed in spring and flower in summer are some of the easiest to grow, requiring little more than moist compost (soil mix) and frost-free conditions. Courgettes, nasturtiums, pot marigolds, salad rocket (arugula),

Above: A harvest of courgette (zucchini) flowers.

runner (green) beans and sunflowers all fall into this category. If you want early flowers, sow indoors in spring, into seed trays or pots and transplant into the final growing positions after all risk of frost has passed. Otherwise, if you don't want to be bothered with the business of

transplanting seedlings, just wait a little longer and sow outdoors, directly into good garden soil. By the time the seedlings have germinated, frosts should have disappeared. If they still threaten, you will have to protect the young seedlings overnight with cloches.

Left: Nasturtiums are easy to grow from seed sown in a propagator or directly into the container where they are to grow. They grow quickly and will soon provide a feast for the eyes and for the table.

Above: Marigolds are also one of the easiest flowers to grow. Parsley is a little more difficult but certainly not impossible.

sowing indoors

COMPARTMENTALIZED TRAYS

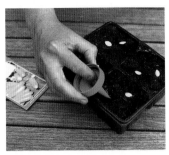

1 △ *Sow courgettes (zucchini) in a moist, good-quality potting compost (planting mix) in compartmentalized seed trays. Sow 2 seeds per pot or compartment, 1cm/½in deep. Place on a warm window-sill, in the greenhouse or in a propagator 16–18°C/ 60–65°F and cover with clear polythene or plastic until the seedlings emerge. After a few days discard the weaker seedling. Keep compost moist at all times.*

2 △ *In spring, harden young plants off by putting them outside in the daytime but bringing them inside during the night-time when temperatures dip. Towards the end of spring or in early summer, when all risk of frost has passed, transplant outside in a sunny spot 60–90cm/2–3ft apart.*

GARDENER'S TIP
This same process could be used for sunflowers, nasturtiums, borage and pot marigolds.

INDIVIDUAL POTS

1 △ *Sow runner (green) beans in a moist, good-quality potting compost (planting mix) in individual pots. Sow 2 seeds per pot or compartment, 4cm/1½in deep. Place on a warm window-sill, in the greenhouse or in a propagator 16–18°C/60–65°F and cover with clear polythene or plastic until the seedlings emerge. After a few days discard the weaker seedling. Keep compost moist, but not sodden, at all times.*

2 △ *In spring, harden plants off by putting them outside in the daytime but bringing them back at night-time when temperatures dip. Towards the end of spring or early summer, when all risk of frost has passed, transplant outside in a sunny spot 60–90cm/2–3ft apart.*

GARDENER'S TIP
This same process could be used for courgettes (zucchini), sunflowers, and nasturtiums.

MINI PROPAGATOR

1 △ *Another way to grow seeds is to sow in a mini propagator where individual cells allow a quantity of seedlings to be germinated, each with a separate root system. This system has a capacity for 40 seeds, allowing for several different plantings. Use a moist, good-quality compost (soil mix) and bring level to within 1cm/½in of the top of the cells. Marigolds and nasturtiums have been planted here.*

2 △ *Place the lid over the compost to create a sheltered and humid environment. Remove the lid once germination has taken place and keep soil moist, but not sodden, at all times. Transplant very carefully, either into containers or into the garden where they are to mature.*

GARDENER'S TIP
This system could be used for borage, dill, and chives as well as many other seeds.

sowing into containers

FROM SEED

1 △ *Sow fine seeds such as salad rocket (arugula) direct into a small to medium container where they can germinate, grow on and mature in the same pot. Use a moist, good-quality potting compost (planting mix) and bring level to within 2.5cm/1in of the top of the container. Scatter seeds over the surface of the compost, cover with a little more compost, and keep moist, but not sodden, in a frost-free environment. The seeds are quick to germinate in warm weather. Thin seedlings ruthlessly so that you are left with only half of the original number sown.*

2 △ *Put the pot in a sunny position and keep the compost moist at all times. The young plants will soon come into flower, and though these flowers are delicate to look at, they are certainly tasty and absolutely delicious. Keep picking them to encourage further flower production.*

COMBINATION PLANTING

1 △ *You can combine different seeds in a large window-box. Try runner (green) beans, tall sunflowers and nasturtiums in a large tub or barrel. Courgettes (zucchini) and nasturtiums can be planted in any medium or large pot. Sow the seeds in pairs into moist multi-purpose potting compost (planting mix) in spring, but protect against frost until late spring. Thin each pair to the strongest seedling.*

Above: A colourful combination of runner (green) beans, nasturtiums and sunflowers.

Above: Sunflowers and nasturtiums sown and flowering together.

sowing into the ground

Plants such as courgettes (zucchini), sunflowers, nasturtiums and runner (green) beans can all be sown outside from mid- to end spring. Plant in pairs, directly into prepared ground in a sunny spot in the garden where you want them to flower. The crop will be slightly later than those started indoors, but they will make rapid growth. It is recommended to sow the seeds slightly deeper than the indoor method. Sow courgettes 2.5cm/1in deep and 60–90cm/2–3ft apart; sunflowers 2.5cm/1in deep and 30cm/12in apart; nasturtiums 1.5cm/½in deep and 25cm/10in apart; and runner beans 5cm/2in deep and 15–22cm/6–9in apart, where they are to grow and fruit. Thin to the strongest seedling. Keep soil moist. Protect if frost threatens young plants. Grow 4–8 plants to produce a good harvest of flowers and, where applicable, fruit.

Pot marigolds, salad rocket (arugula), borage and basil can also be sown outside. Prepare the soil well, raking it to a fine tilth, and then sow in small patches or in lines at a depth of 1.5cm/½in. Basil will germinate easier with additional warmth or left until early Summer. Thin seedlings to 25–30cm/10–12in between plants.

self-seeding

Many plants will self-seed if allowed. Some are hardy plants which will survive frosty winters and will either live for many years (perennials) or flower in their second year (biennials). Cowslips, primroses, violets and double daisies will multiply regularly once grown in the garden, as will evening primrose, hollyhocks, sweet cicely, fennel and marjoram.

Others are hardy annuals which will grow from seed ripened the previous summer which has fallen to the ground

Above: *Cowslips self-seed in grasslands and borders.*

in the autumn. Some will sprout before the winter sets in, others will wait until the following spring. Marigolds and borage will often flower in this way, re-newing themselves year after year.

Some plants cast their ripe seed immediately around their roots where the new seedlings sprout and grow on, often unnoticed. You will often find young cowslips in the grass or border around the parent plant. Others throw their seed to the wind and appear in a completely different part of the garden or even in someone else's garden. Dandelions are prime examples and are notable for their invasions. Others have their hard seeds carried by birds to new territory. How otherwise can we explain the presence of dog roses and elderflower bushes in so many gardens and hedgerows?

saving seeds

The seeds of some plants will be destroyed by frost and therefore will not be able to self-seed in some environments. Sunflowers, nasturtiums, runner (green) beans and rocket (arugula) must all be collected and saved in order to supply the seeds for the following year.

In other cases, where the plants are hardy, you may want to harvest the seed crop yourself in order to prevent birds and animals from helping themselves and eliminating those left for nature's natural methods. You might simply want to gather the seeds so that you can grow them in a controlled environment, or you might want to give them away to friends. Wait until they are ripe. Then gather on a dry day and place in a sealed brown bag. Label clearly and keep in a cool, dry place. Sow the seeds the following spring.

prevention of self-seeding

Some plants have such prolific seeds that you may want to cut the seed-heads off in order to prevent an invasion. Sweet cicely, angelica and evening primrose might all fall into this category, particularly if you have grown them for a year or two and have had a good stock of plants. Simply remove the seed-heads before they are ready to shed their seeds. Angelica seed-heads make good dried-flower arrangements.

Above: *Remove angelica seed heads before they ripen to prevent too many seedlings the following spring.*

Cuttings and divisions

Some plants such as alpine pinks, lavender, lemon verbena and geraniums are easy to propagate by taking cuttings. You will need to choose strong non-flowering side shoots.

You will soon be able to propagate these plants many times over and create an entire new stock of plants.

Above: *Take lavender cuttings in autumn.*

how to take cuttings

SCENTED ALPINE PINKS
Dianthus

1 △ *In mid- to late summer, select strong side shoots from alpine pinks, 8–10cm/ 3–4in long. Remove lower leaves and dip the cut end into hormone rooting powder (optional). Tap gently to remove excess powder.*

2 △ *Use a dibber to insert the cuttings into a small pot filled with moist potting compost (planting mix), covered with a thin layer of dry sand. As the dibber makes the hole, the dry sand trickles downwards making a good medium for the base of the cutting to root into. Firm the cuttings into the compost and keep in a shaded position. Spray daily with a fine mist.*

3 *The cuttings should have established good roots in about 3–4 weeks. Remove the cuttings from the pot and place individually in 8cm/3in pots of potting compost. Grow on until late autumn and plant out into their flowering positions or grow over the winter in a cold greenhouse and plant out in spring.*

LAVENDER
Lavendula

1 △ *In autumn take 12.5cm/5in heel cuttings, pulling the small branch away from the main stem with a heel of woody growth attached. Dip the heel into hormone rooting powder (optional). Tap gently to remove excess powder.*

2 △ *Use a dibber to insert the cuttings into a small pot filled with moist potting compost (planting mix), covered with a thin layer of dry sand. Place the pot in a shaded position or in a cold greenhouse. Mist daily. Keep compost barely moist as the root system develops.*

3 *Roots should have formed within 4 weeks. Keep over the winter in a protected area such as a cold frame and plant out the next spring into flowering positions.*

SCENTED GERANIUMS
Pelargonium

1 △ *Take 5–10cm/2–4in tip cuttings in spring or autumn. The length of the cuttings will very much depend on whether they are short- or long-jointed. Prepare 8–10cm/3–4in pots of seed compost (soil mix) mixed with grit (gravel) or perlite. Water well and drain. Add a thin layer of dry sand on top. Remove lower leaves from the cuttings.*

2 △ *Dip into hormone rooting powder (optional) and using a dibber, insert the cuttings into the compost. As the dibber makes the hole, the dry sand trickles downwards making a good medium for the base of the cutting to root into. Place cuttings on a window-sill or in a greenhouse. Keep in a light, but shaded position, out of full sun. The top growth needs to be kept dry, with the compost moist. When rooted, normally after about 3 weeks, pot the cuttings on into individual 9cm/ 3½in pots using a good potting compost (planting mix). Scented geraniums are not hardy and will not tolerate frost.*

MINTS
Mentha species

1 △ *From late spring through the summer take tip cuttings of various types of mint and insert them in water where they will form roots in just a matter of days.*

2 △ *Remove the lower leaves and insert the stems in water in a narrow-necked bottle. Put the bottle in a light, shaded position, inside or out, and keep the water level topped up.*

3 *When the roots have formed, pot up individually into small 8cm/3in pots.*

ROSES
Rosa

1 *Take 23–30cm/9–12in cuttings, with a heel of strong, non-flowering lateral shoots in late summer and early autumn. Strip off all leaves, except two or three at the top of each cutting and also remove the buds in the leaf axils. Choose a partially shaded place in the garden, not directly overhung by trees, and take out a V-shaped trench 15–20cm/ 6–8in deep.*

2 *Fill the bottom 2.5cm/1in with horticultural sand. After dibbing the cuttings in a root-forming hormone powder, insert them a few centimetres/inches apart in the sand.*

3 *Firm the soil over the cuttings and water the foliage. If the weather is dry, water the whole trench thoroughly. Plant out in their permanent position the following autumn.*

divisions

Many plants such as lemon balm, marjoram, bergamot, chives, day lilies, cowslips and primroses can be propagated in spring by digging them up from the garden and carefully dividing the roots. Often, several new plants can be made from one large clump. Pot the individual new plants into pots where they can be grown on or replant them straight into the garden.

As an alternative to tip cuttings, mint can also be propagated by division. Sometimes it is necessary to sever a shared root, but any piece of root will soon re-establish itself. Pots of mint can be divided easily into two clumps once one of the main roots is cut. Pot the two halves on into new compost (soil mix) or plant directly in the garden.

violets **primroses** cowslips

daisies rosemary **sweet cicely**

chives **marigolds** anchusa

alpine pinks thyme **sage**

lemon verbena **geraniums**

day lilies **elderflower** borage

roses lavender **nasturtium**

hollyhocks evening primrose

bergamot sunflower

basil mint hyssop

marjoram

Plant
Directory

The list of edible flowering plants is long, and allows almost everyone, whether they garden with beds and borders or just with containers, to grow a wide variety to eat during the spring and summer months. Many of these flowers have been eaten for centuries and offer a delicious and attractive addition to our diets.

Right: A mixed herb trough can be enjoyed for the flowers as much as the foliage, both in the garden and the kitchen.

Complementary Foods and Flowers

Below are a few suggestions for food and flower combinations. Experiment with others depending on the season.

marjoram

hyssop

Beef with marjoram and sweet rocket
Chicken with thyme, hyssop and lavender
Fish with bergamot, fennel and dill
Lamb with rosemary, lavender and mint jelly
Pork sausages with chives, marjoram and sage
Fish sauces with pot marigolds, fennel, chive and dill

borage

Mustards with sage, dill, fennel and salad rocket (arugula)
Baked potatoes with pot marigolds and chives
Mushrooms with thyme and chives
Pasta with pot marigolds, courgette (zucchini) flowers, sunflowers and chives
Salads with primroses, violets, borage, sweet cicely, chives, pot marigolds, nasturtiums, sweet rocket, bergamot, evening primrose and mint
Tomatoes with basil and marjoram

sunflower

courgette (zucchini) flower

Bread with sunflower and lavender
Cakes, meringues and **desserts** with crystallized primroses, violets, violas, cowslips, rosemary, rose, pinks, borage and anchusa
Fritters or **batters** with courgette (zucchini) flowers, nasturtiums, clary sage and elderflowers
Fruit salads with borage, hollyhock, mint and evening primrose
Honey with cowslips, lavender and roses
Ice creams with roses, mint flowers and lavender, **sorbets** with roses and fennel
Ice cubes with borage, scented geraniums, roses, alpine pinks, anchusa and violets
Scones with strawberry and elderflower jam or lavender jelly

complementary foods and flowers

violas

geraniums

day lily

hollyhocks

purple basil

Beer with **hops** and **dandelion**

Syrup with **cowslips** and **violets, roses** and **mint**

Tea with **lime blossom, hyssop, lavender, clover, chamomile,
sweet woodruff, hibiscus, mint** and **lemon verbena**

Wines with **elderflower, cowslips, lime blossom, dandelion, mint,
primrose, clary sage, hop, sweet woodruff** and **clover**

Butters with **thyme, sage, pot marigold, hyssop** and **chives**
sweet butter with **roses, alpine pinks** and **violets**

Oils with **marjoram, mint, lavender, bergamot, sage, thyme, hyssop**
and **fennel**

Vinegars with **mint, violets, chives, rose**
and **nasturtium**

chamomile

Above: borage and marigold petal salad.

The following plant directory includes plants that have been used in cooking for hundreds, and in some cases thousands, of years. However, it is important to be aware that there might be detrimental individual reactions to these flowers.

Some people may react against the pollen that the flowers produce. Always remove any excess, and if in doubt remove all the pollen-bearing parts. Obviously if there is a known hypersensitivity, then avoid eating the flowers altogether, as each one will automatically produce some pollen, although some will create a lot more than others.

The list of edible flowers shown here is not all-embracing but it does offer a wide choice. Use it with discretion and enjoy the results.

Alcea rosea
HOLLYHOCKS

Hollyhocks are short-lived perennials, generally flowering the second year although some hybrids can be treated as annuals. They are thought to derive from temperate parts of western Asia. They grow 1.5–2.5m/5–8ft tall and have a succession of large papery yellow, white, red, pink or dark purple flowers throughout the summer. Hollyhocks are a favourite of bees, and because of this, care must be taken when picking them in the garden. Remove leaves if any signs of rust develop. It doesn't affect the flowers.

- SITE Well-drained soil in full sun. Excellent at the back of a border and for a cottage garden. They will need staking in exposed places.
- PROPAGATION Sow seed for annuals in seed trays either in late winter, or *in situ* where they are to flower in spring. For biennials sow seeds in mid-summer. They can be transplanted in autumn. They will happily self-seed, often in the most unexpected places.
- CULINARY USES The flowers can be crystallized and used on cakes, mousses and roulades or mix them with salad leaves for a stunning dish.
- FLOWER DISSECTION Take newly opened flowers, and remove the central reproductive parts. Cut off any greenery and brush off all traces of pollen. You will be left with five separate petals, to be eaten individually.

Allium schoenoprasum
CHIVES

Bulbous perennial from Europe, Asia and North America, often eaten for its long cylindrical onion-flavoured leaves as well as its pale purple flower-heads. Umbels of up to 30 or 40 bell-shaped, purple flowers may be produced on a single stem in late spring and early summer. Clumps of chives may grow 30cm/12in high and 25–35cm/10–14in across.

- SITE Sun or shade.
- PROPAGATION Sow in spring, direct in the garden or in containers. Divide clumps in spring, replanting groups of 6–10 bulbs.
- CULINARY USES Chive flowers have a mild onion flavour and are surprisingly crunchy. They can be widely used on potatoes and carrots, in salads, and salad dressing, tossed in pastas, omelettes and scrambled eggs, used to create decorations on pâtés and mixed as chive butter. They can be cooked to make a white fish sauce or added to a cheese sauce for extra bite. They can be used to make chive vinegar. The starry white flowers of garlic chives, *Allium tuberosum*, can be used in the same way, although the flavour is slightly more of garlic than onion.
- FLOWER DISSECTION Pick the freshest flower-heads. Remove green stalks and snip the individual flowers off in small groups. Use a few or in large amounts.

Allium schoenoprasum (chives)

Above: *Lavender and roses.*

Aloysia triphylla
LEMON VERBENA

Half-hardy, deciduous shrub from Chile and Argentina which grows up to 3m/10ft high and wide. It was introduced to Europe by the Spanish in the 17th century who grew it to make perfumed oil. Its tapering leaves are very rough, but just one touch is enough to release the distinctive lemon fragrance which remains powerful whether the leaves are fresh or dried. Long panicles of tiny white flowers are borne in summer, dainty but not showy.

- SITE It needs a dry, sunny position and protection under glass in frosty conditions.
- PROPAGATION Root softwood cuttings in summer.
- CULINARY USES Both the flowers and leaves have an extremely strong lemon fragrance which can be used to flavour jellies, ice cream, cakes and drinks. The leaves can either be cut fine when very young and mixed in with the recipe, or used for flavour and then extracted before eating. For example, leaves can be placed on the base of a sponge cake or stewed with apples and removed after cooking.
- FLOWER DISSECTION The flowers are very small and do not retain their colour for long once picked. Harvest them just before serving, leaving all green parts behind.

Aloysia triphylla (lemon verbena)

Anchusa azurea
ANCHUSA

Anchusa is a tall perennial from dry sunny sites in southern Europe, North Africa and western Asia which will grow up to 1m/3ft high and 60cm/2ft across. Its bright blue flowers are borne in early summer. Its leaves are very hairy, like those of borage, a close relative. Cut back flower stems after flowering to encourage further production the same season.

- SITE Sunny. It is a clump-forming plant which is useful towards the back of a flower border or in a large container.
- PROPAGATION Sow seeds in spring. Anchusa is a short-lived perennial. To prolong its life, cut back all top growth after the second flowering. This will encourage the formation of basal rosettes which will last over the winter and will provide a strong plant for the following year.
- CULINARY USES The flowers have a wonderful blue colouring and the flavour of lettuce. They can be used in many decorative ways with pink shellfish, salmon, avocado or melon, for example. Mix them with marigold petals or oranges for a vibrant flowery salad. They can also be crystallized and used to decorate cakes and creamy desserts or frozen in ice cubes.
- FLOWER DISSECTION Each flower has five petals and is about 1.5cm /½in across. Remove the petals intact from all the green parts.

Anethum graveolens
DILL

Dill probably originated in southwest Asia and India but is now widely naturalized in Europe and North America. Sown in spring, it grows 60cm/24in high and 30cm/12in wide. By mid-summer, it produces flattened umbels of tiny yellow flowers 9cm/3½in across on tall, hollow ridged stems. The thread-like blue-green leaves are strongly aromatic.

- SITE Sunny well-drained site, either in containers or the garden. May need pea sticks or other supports as they can be rather floppy. If grown near to fennel the flavour becomes less intense. Beware of slugs.
- PROPAGATION Sow seed *in situ* at monthly intervals from late spring throughout the summer.
- CULINARY USES Dill flowers have a similar flavour to the leaves and make a lovely addition to many salads, vegetables, fish dishes, and associated mayonnaises. Mix the flowers and leaves into a hot white sauce flavoured with white wine vinegar and sugar to which a little cream and egg yolk may be added. It is delicious to eat with baked ham or poached fish. Dill flowers can be added to lots of pickles including cucumber and cauliflower as well as, or instead of, the dill seeds.
- FLOWER DISSECTION Remove the stalks and use the flowers whole.

Anethum graveolens (dill)

plant directory

plant directory

Bellis perennis
DAISY

The daisy is a very common evergreen perennial from the grasslands of Europe which now has rich pink, white and deep red garden cultivars. These are usually treated as biennial and are perfect for use as spring bedding in formal gardens. The flowers will self-seed with abandon, if allowed, making a surprising addition to the perfect lawn. The flowers are produced in large numbers, about 15cm/6in high, from early spring to early summer. Plants will grow about 25cm/10in across.

- SITE Sun or light shade. Grow in containers or in the garden.
- PROPAGATION Either sow seeds in pots or compartmentalized seed trays in spring and later transfer the young plants to the garden or sow direct where they are to flower. Once established, divide in early spring or after flowering. They will self-seed.
- CULINARY USES The flowers are not particularly strong tasting, but the petals make an interesting garnish for all manner of desserts and savoury dishes. Use to decorate cakes, cookies, mousses and pâtés. Toss young leaves and flower quills in salads. The roots were commonly eaten in country areas in Italy and Spain.
- FLOWER DISSECTION Gently pull the petals (or quills) from the flower-head. You will have masses from just one flower-head.

Bellis perennis (daisy)

Borago officinalis
BORAGE

Borage is a hardy annual plant native to Europe. It will grow 60cm/24in high and 45cm/18in across. The star-shaped flowers, 2.5cm/1in across, are produced over many weeks in summer on thick, hairy stems.

- SITE Full sun or partial shade. It is a loosely branching plant which is perfect for any cottage or herb garden. Can be grown in any large container.
- PROPAGATION Sow seeds in the garden in spring after all danger of frost has passed. Once established in the garden it will self-seed.
- CULINARY USES The flowers are a gorgeous blue and look wonderful in ice cubes, crystallized on cakes, in a savoury jelly, as a decoration on pâté or a green salad, or floating on a bowl of punch. The stems can be cut, peeled and added to salads to give the flavour of cucumber.
- FLOWER DISSECTION Each flower has five petals with a group of prominent black stamens which should come away together, intact, from the hairy green parts. The petals have a cucumber taste and the stamens add a sweet edge.

COOK'S TIP
For asthma sufferers or those with pollen allergies, it is easy to remove the stamens of the borage flower.

Calendula officinalis
POT MARIGOLD

This marigold is not to be confused with *Tagetes*, sometimes known as African marigold. Pot marigold is a fast-growing hardy annual from Europe which reaches 60cm/24in high and across. It produces a bright array of orange, yellow, cream or apricot flowers which may be up to 10cm/4in across. Deadhead regularly to encourage a long succession of flowers.

- SITE Sun or partial shade in well-drained soil. Ideal for creating a bright and cheery display in the border or in containers.
- PROPAGATION Sow seed in early spring where it is to grow. You will find it self-seeds generously and provides early flowers for the following year.
- CULINARY USES The slightly peppery tasting petals, the long period of availability and the intense colour of the pot marigold make it a very popular culinary flower. It used to be dried in large quantities to flavour soups and stews throughout the winter months. It was also made into conserves, syrups and wine, baked in puddings, preserved in oils, pickled in vinegar or used to flavour and colour butter.
- FLOWER DISSECTION Choose the freshest flowers and pull the long petals away from the flower-head in small groups. They can be dried.

Calendula officinalis (pot marigold)

Chamaemelum nobile
CHAMOMILE

Chamomile is a mat-forming perennial 30cm/12in by 45cm/18in which produces white flowers in summer. Traditionally, this plant was used to create scented seats which were wonderfully aromatic when used. 'Treneague' is the modern cultivar now used for this purpose as it is lower than the species and spreads more rapidly. However, this type does not flower.

* SITE Full sun. Light, well-drained soil.
* PROPAGATION Divide in spring or sow seed in pots in spring.
* CULINARY USES Chamomile is valued for its sweet apple-scented leaves which release a very pleasing fragrance, especially when crushed. Apart from chamomile tea and chamomile wine, they can be added to bath water to relieve sunburn or used to make a rinse for fair hair. Chamomile flower oil was recommended for this purpose as early as the 16th century. The flowers are extremely bitter to taste raw.
* FLOWER DISSECTION Each daisy-like flower, about 1.5cm/½in across, has many petals. When making tea use the whole flower-head. The taste is bitter so use them sparingly, sweetening to taste with honey if desired. Chamomile tea is known and enjoyed for its sleep-inducing qualities.

Cichorium intybus
CHICORY (BELGIAN ENDIVE)

This hardy, clump-forming perennial comes from the dry, sunny grassland areas of the Mediterranean. It likes chalk and limestone soils and can grow as high as 1.2m/4ft by 60cm/2ft across. The blue dandelion-like flowers appear in summer and may occasionally be white or pink.

* SITE Dry and sunny.
* PROPAGATION Sow seeds in a cold frame in spring or autumn.
* CULINARY USES The flower buds can be pickled, while the petals are a beautiful addition to any salad. They have a lettuce-like flavour. Chicory has a large tap root which can be roasted and ground as a coffee substitute. Young roots can be boiled and eaten as a vegetable. Young leaves may be eaten in salads uncooked. The chicons, which are the blanched heads produced by forcing the roots in warmth and darkness, are often sold for salads.
* FLOWER DISSECTION The beautiful, clear blue-fluted petals should be removed from the flower-head leaving all green parts behind.

> **WARNING**
> Contact with all parts of the plant can irritate the skin or aggravate skin allergies.

Cichorium intybus (chicory)

Citrus sinensis and Citrus limon
CITRUS

These small, spiny evergreen trees originate in southeast Asia and the islands of the east Pacific. The flowers are produced from spring to summer, either singly or in small groups. Each beautiful, white, fragrant five-petalled flower is about 4–5cm/1½–2in across. The fruit takes a year to mature.

* SITE Full sun; needs to be kept over the winter in frost-free conditions. Best planted in a large container which can be placed outside during the summer but withdrawn to a conservatory or greenhouse during the colder months. Citrus trees grow in neutral or slightly acidic soil.
* PROPAGATION Root semi-ripe cuttings in summer. Seed can be sown but seedlings rarely come true to the parent. New plants will take many years to flower.
* CULINARY USES The scent of the flowers is both sweet and powerful and the flavour is excellent. They are ideal for crystallizing. They would be wonderful used to decorate the top of a lemon sponge gâteau or lemon torte. Orange blossom was once the glory of a bridal wreath and would be a wonderful way to decorate a wedding cake. Citrus flowers can also be preserved in syrup and used to flavour oil.
* FLOWER DISSECTION Pick newly opened flowers, but remove any green parts. If you are sensitive to pollen just eat the petals.

Crocus sativus
SAFFRON

This is a bulb which flowers in autumn and grows 30–45cm/12–18in high. It looks like a crocus with its rich, lilac funnel-shaped flowers, each with dark purple veins. Each corm produces between one and five flowers.

- SITE Saffron needs a hot, dry summer to produce flowers and is ideally suited to the Spanish climate where it grows. It was grown in enormous quantities for over 200 years around Saffron Walden, in Essex, England. Indeed, the town derived its name from the flower.
- PROPAGATION Plant dry bulbs in autumn. Break off outer corms and replant in late summer.
- CULINARY USES Use the styles to flavour and colour rice, soups, bread, cakes and cookies. In the past it was used to flavour herbal liqueurs, as well as meat and fish dishes. With so many uses, it is not surprising to find that it used to be considered an aphrodisiac. Nowadays it can be obtained easily in its dried form, although it is one of the most expensive of spices. A cheaper option would be to buy the dry bulbs to plant in the autumn.
- FLOWER DISSECTION It is the deep-red three-pronged style which is removed and used for culinary purposes. Only a very small amount is required to obtain a deep yellow colour.

Crocus sativus (saffron)

Cucurbita pepo var. Courgette or Marrow
COURGETTE (ZUCCHINI)

Courgettes (zucchini) are grown as a summer vegetable. They soon grow into large plants about 60cm/2ft or more high and wide. Keep well fed and watered.

- SITE Sunny and moist.
- PROPAGATION Sow seeds in little pots on a kitchen window-sill or greenhouse in early spring and plant outside in the garden or large containers once all risk of frost has passed.
- CULINARY USES Courgette flowers can be eaten hot or cold. Try the Provençal method of cooking them in a tomato sauce and then served on a bed of spinach, or eat them cold, stuffed with cooked rice, herbs, dried fruit, nuts, meat or fish mixed with a mayonnaise sauce.
- FLOWER DISSECTION Courgettes and marrows (large zucchini) produce both female and male flowers. The female flowers are on short stems with the embryo fruit behind, while the male flowers are on longer stems. By cutting the female flowers you will curtail fruit production. Depending on how many plants you have growing, choose the male flowers to harvest out of preference to allow the courgette crops to grow. Pick flowers when they are dry and fully open, removing all green parts. Check them carefully for insects before using. Earwigs and tiny beetles may be lurking but are easily washed off.

Dianthus
ALPINE PINK

There are many species and hybrids of alpine pink which share the same delicious clove-like fragrance. Colours vary from white through to pink, lilac, cerise and purple, often with different coloured margins and centres which makes them even more attractive. These include the taller old-fashioned kinds such as white 'Mrs Sinkins', popular post-war hybrids such as pale pink 'Doris' and all the dwarf alpine cultivars such as pink 'Whatfield Can-Can' and pink and ruby-red 'Betty Norton'. They are all evergreen perennials, although some may live only a few years before they need replacing.

- SITE All prefer a sunny position with neutral to alkaline soil.
- PROPAGATION Take cuttings from non-flowering shoots in summer and pot up in a gritty (gravelly) compost (soil mix). Pot on or plant out in autumn.
- CULINARY USES Many alpine pinks and carnations have a clove-like fragrance which makes them very suitable for flavouring sugar, oils and vinegars. They can be crystallized and used to decorate cakes and meringues. In medieval times they were used to flavour wines hence the old fashioned variety 'Sops in Wine'.
- FLOWER DISSECTION Carefully detach each petal from the flower-head. Remove the white heel at the base of the petal as it has a bitter taste.

Dianthus (alpine pink)

Eruca vescaria ssp. sativa
SALAD ROCKET (ARUGULA)

This fast-maturing annual grows 60cm/
2ft tall and bears a succession of heavily
veined, pale yellow flowers which turn to
white with age.

- SITE Sun or partial shade, but moist. The
  sunnier the site the more flowers will be
  produced. Keep picking them off in order
  to prolong production through the
  summer.
- PROPAGATION Sow from seed in late
  spring, either directly in the borders
  where they are to grow or in medium-
  sized containers. Thin after two or three
  weeks. For a succession of crops, sow at
  one-monthly intervals.
- CULINARY USES The leaves and flowers
  are marvellous for adding a zingy bite to
  any salad, particularly where strong,
  gutsy flavours are appreciated. Rocket,
  purslane and lettuce is a traditional salad
  combination. The flowers can be
  preserved in oils, vinegar and butter.
  Rocket butter with steak and mushrooms
  is a real treat.
- FLOWER DISSECTION This is a simple,
  four-petalled flower which can be
  removed from the stem with or without
  the semi-ripe seed capsule behind. The
  seed capsule is packed with a very strong
  peppery flavour and makes the flower
  extremely tasty.

Foeniculum vulgare
FENNEL

Deep-rooted perennial which is native to
southern Europe where it thrives on poor
soil and dry summers. It grows 1.8m/6ft
tall by 45cm/18in across. In late summer,
its slender, branching stems bear thread-
like leaves and support the many umbels,
10cm/4in across, of tiny yellow flowers
which have the same characteristic sweet
aniseed flavour of the leaves and stems.
There is a handsome bronze form called
Foeniculum vulgare 'Purpureum'. This can
be used in exactly the same way as the
common green variety.

- SITE Sunny, well-drained soil. It looks
  wonderful in a herb garden, amidst
  cottage borders and in large containers.
- PROPAGATION The plant is not long lived
  and may need replanting after three
  years. Divide plants in autumn or sow
  seed in late spring, after all risk of frost
  has passed, direct where it is to grow.
  It is very good at self-seeding.
- CULINARY USES Both the root, leaves,
  seeds and flowers are edible. Cold
  salmon, pâtés and salads are also greatly
  enhanced by the addition of both leaves
  and flowers. The flowers may be kept for
  winter use preserved in oil, vinegar or
  butter or use the flowers and semi-ripe
  seeds to pickle cucumbers or when
  making sauerkraut.
- FLOWER DISSECTION Pick newly opened
  flower-heads and cut off the main stalk.

Foeniculum vulgare (fennel)

Fuchsia arborescens
FUCHSIA

Fuchsia arborescens is known as the lilac
fuchsia because its flowers are similar in
colour to the common lilac. Native to
Mexico and Central America, it makes an
upright, evergreen shrub or small tree
growing up to 2m/6ft by 1.7m/5½ft.
It requires a minimum temperature of
5°C/41°F. The tiny slender flowers, only
1.5cm/½in long, appear in one flush in
summer. Replant into a larger pot in
the spring.

- SITE Full sun with moisture. Ideal in
  containers which can be kept during the
  winter in a warm conservatory or
  greenhouse.
- PROPAGATION Root softwood cuttings in
  spring or sow seeds at
  15–24°C/59–75°F in spring.
- CULINARY USES These tiny flowers could
  be added to any salad dish and would
  enhance a fish pâté. All fuchsia flowers
  and fruit are edible although some are
  less sweet than others. The very
  flamboyant types used in summer
  bedding schemes are not strong in
  flavour, but they would look sensational
  crystallized and used on a summer cake
  or fruit mousse. They could be floated on
  a fruit salad.
- FLOWER DISSECTION The newly opened
  flowers have a very sweet flavour.
  Remove the tiny flower intact from the
  stalk and eat whole.

Galium odoratum
SWEET WOODRUFF

Sweet woodruff is a very pretty carpeting perennial from the woodlands of Europe, north Africa and Russia. The flowers grow in clusters, about 20cm/8in high, like tiny white stars held above whorls of elongated leaves. They appear in late spring and early summer. Plants will spread indefinitely, but the roots do not grow deeply and are easily removed.

- SITE Moist shade. With its frothy display of tiny white flowers, it makes an ideal border along paths in a north-facing garden, or it may be grown in containers. It is excellent dug up and used as a living liner in hanging baskets.
- PROPAGATION Divide in early spring or after flowering.
- CULINARY USES Both leaves and flowers are used as a flavouring in making wine. In Germany, it is used with sparkling white wine, in France with champagne and in Switzerland it is steeped in Cognac or Benedictine. Crushed or dried leaves smell of new-mown hay and are used to scent rooms. Woodruff tea can be made from the whole plant using flowers and leaves. Pour a pint of boiling water on a large handful.
- FLOWER DISSECTION The flower is rather bitter eaten on its own, but it is used extensively in Europe as a wine flavouring. The whole flower, stalk and leaves can be used.

Galium odoratum (sweet woodruff)

Helianthus annuus
SUNFLOWER

This is a fast-growing, tall, branching annual from the sunny summer regions of North America. Sunflowers can reach 5m/15ft high and up to 60cm/2ft across with large circular flowers from late summer to early autumn. There are some dwarf varieties such as 'Pacino', 30cm/12in tall, and 'Sunspot' 60cm/24in tall. Although yellow is still dominant, a variety of shades are now available including the dark mahogany-red 'Velvet Queen' and pale yellow 'Lemon Queen'.

- SITE Full sun, sheltered from strong winds.
- PROPAGATION Sow seeds in spring. Either sow inside in individual pots from which the young seedlings can be transplanted when all threat of frost has passed, or sow directly in garden soil or pots where they are to flower. Tall varieties will need staking.
- CULINARY USES The buds can be eaten whole. Blanch in salted boiling water for two minutes to kill any insects and remove any bitter flavours, then rinse and return to fresh boiling water for another three minutes. Toss in garlic butter. The petals can be eaten uncooked in salads and pasta or stir fries. The seeds may be shelled and eaten raw.
- FLOWER DISSECTION Cut off the buds and use whole. Harvest the petals just before cooking, pulling them away gently from the centre. Leave the seeds to mature to be harvested at a later date.

Hemerocallis
DAY LILY

This is a clump-forming perennial from the marshy river valleys and meadowlands of Japan, China and Korea. The strappy, dark green leaves reach from 23–120cm/9–48in depending on variety, and the flowers usually grow slightly taller. The flowers last for only one day, hence their name, but each plant has a succession of blooms which extends over a period of several weeks in summer. The flowers are trumpet shaped and may be 15cm/6in or more across. Orange is the most common colour although petals may be white, yellow, pink, red or dark purple.

- SITE Moist, sunny site in garden soil or, if small varieties are grown, in containers.
- PROPAGATION Divide clumps in spring. This task should be done every second or third year in order to maintain vigour.
- CULINARY USES The buds and flowers are both crunchy, with a wonderful flavour of mangetouts (snow peas) but with a delicious peppery aftertaste. They have been eaten in China for centuries and are excellent in stir fries, soups and salads. The petals add a rich variety of colour to any dish. Eat in moderation as they have been known to have a laxative and diuretic effect if consumed in large quantities.
- FLOWER DISSECTION Both buds and petals can be eaten – just remove all stems before use.

Hemerocallis (day lily)

Hesperis matronalis
SWEET ROCKET

Also known as Dame's violet, this is a short-lived perennial from southern Europe, Siberia, and western and central Asia. It blooms from late spring to summer, producing panicles of white, pale lilac or purple cross-shaped flowers in great numbers. It is highly scented in the evening and a favourite nectar food for insects. It grows 1m/3ft high and 45cm/18in wide. It can become unruly and is better staked or supported with a wicker wigwam (teepee).

- SITE Sun or partial shade, on neutral or alkaline soil. Perfect for the cottage garden or among a planting of old-fashioned shrub roses.
- PROPAGATION Easily grown from seed sown in spring. Once grown in the borders it will self-seed generously.
- CULINARY USES Young leaves have a similar, but stronger, taste to salad rocket, and can be used in salads. The flowers taste mildly of lettuce, which makes them suitable for decoration of many different salads, pâtés and fish dishes. They can be preserved for winter use in oil or vinegar.
- FLOWER DISSECTION The flowers can be eaten whole, but first remove the stalk and any greenery. The flowers can be crystallized and used to decorate any number of sweet dishes from cakes and cookies to fruit desserts.

Hibiscus rosa-sinensis
HIBISCUS

This plant is also known as the Rose of China and probably originated in tropical Asia. It forms a small, rounded, bushy evergreen tree 2.5–5m/8–15ft by 1.5–3m/5–10ft. In the wild the species flowers are large, up to 10cm/4in across, with five beautifully formed crimson petals, surrounding pronounced red stamens. There are now many cultivars with many shades of either pink, orange, yellow or white flowers, some either semi-double or double. All the flowers are showy, and although short-lived, a constant supply of new buds means there is a long flowering period.

- SITE Full sun with winter protection. Neutral to slightly acid soil. Minimum temperature is 10–13ºC/50–55ºF.
- PROPAGATION Take semi-ripe cuttings in summer.
- CULINARY USES Hibiscus flowers make a very popular tea. Simply take one flower and add a cup of hot water. Leave to infuse for about four minutes, then strain. The hibiscus petals impart a mild citrus flavour that is complemented by the refreshing addition of rosemary. This combination is also thought to be an aphrodisiac.
- FLOWER DISSECTION Take newly opened flowers and remove the petals from the flower-heads or use whole, though beware of the pollen.

Hibiscus rosa-sinensis (hibiscus)

Humulus lupulus
HOPS

The hop plant grows in many temperate areas of the northern hemisphere, although its country of origin is unknown. It is a vigorous climbing perennial, reaching 6m/20ft, which dies back to the roots every autumn, and grows again quickly the next spring. Small male and female flowers are borne on separate plants in mid- and late summer. 'Aureus' is a gold-leaved variety.

- SITE Sun or partial shade. Hops will grow in woodland, or hedgerows, and can be trained up walls or pergolas. They need support.
- PROPAGATION Root softwood cuttings in spring. Seedlings will appear, but even though they may have originated from the golden variety they will usually be green-leaved.
- CULINARY USES The petals of the female flowers are dried and then used to make hop wine or to flavour home-made beer or mead. The small male flowers are eaten like asparagus. Boil the tips and shoots in salt water with a few drops of lemon juice, and then toss in butter.
- FLOWER DISSECTION The fragrant female flowers appear in cone-shaped green heads which dangle from the branches. They are gathered in late summer and used entire. The male flowers are branched catkins. They are gathered before being fully opened and cooked as a vegetable.

plant directory

Hyssopsus officinalis
HYSSOP

This is an aromatic shrubby plant from southern Europe which grows 60cm/2ft high and 1m/3ft across, although regular trimming can help to contain it. From mid-summer to autumn it produces tall slender spikes of funnel-shaped dark blue flowers which are about 1.5cm/½in long. They can also be white, purple or pink. Butterflies and bees find them very attractive as a source of food.

- SITE Light sandy or alkaline soil with sun or partial shade. Hyssop was traditionally used as an edging plant around borders. Lovely in a formal garden, in a herb bed or in a cottage garden. It can also be grown in containers.
- PROPAGATION Sow seeds in autumn or early spring. Cuttings should be taken in early summer from non-flowering stems.
- CULINARY USES Hyssop tops and flowers were used in soups and salads, and hyssop tea and syrup were common cordials. Hyssop aids digestion of fatty fish and meats and makes an interesting addition to salad dressing. Use the flowers to flavour vinegar and butter. It can also be used in fruit sauces such as cranberry sauce, or put 1.25ml/¼ tsp beneath a peach or apricot pie crust.
- FLOWER DISSECTION Gently pull flowers away from the stem as soon as flowering begins. For a lighter flavour, remove any green parts.

Hyssopsus officinalis (hyssop)

Lavandula angustifolia
LAVENDER

Lavender is a bushy perennial plant with aromatic grey-green leaves which grows about 1m/3ft high and 1.2m/4ft across depending on the variety. It is native to dry, sunny, rocky places in the Mediterranean. Tubular, two-lipped flowers are highly fragrant and packed with nectar, making them very attractive to bees. They are produced on tall, dense spikes and may be dark purple ('Hidcote'), blue-purple ('Munstead'), pink ('Loddon Pink') or white ('Nana Alba').

- SITE Sunny borders among old-fashioned roses, beside a path or in containers.
- PROPAGATION Sow seeds in a cold frame in spring or take semi-ripe cuttings in summer.
- CULINARY USES There are many ways to use lavender flowers, both sweet and savoury. In the past, lavender sugar was used to flavour cookies, sorbets and jelly. It is also used to flavour chicken, sometimes mixing Provençal herbs such as thyme and marjoram as well. The flowers can also be preserved in oil, or used to make tea.
- FLOWER DISSECTION The flowers themselves are small but numerous. Depending on usage, either leave flowers on the stem, carefully remove them, or pluck away the flowers themselves leaving any blue calyx parts behind. Gather when newly opened.

Lilium lancifolium (formerly *L. tigrinum*)
TIGER LILY

The tiger lily is a popular stem-rooting lily from a wide region including Japan, China and Korea. It grows 0.6–1.5m/2–5ft tall and bears up to 40 unscented turkscap flowers in late summer and early autumn, in vibrant orange-red with dark purple spots. 'Enchantment' is a closely related 'Asiatic' hybrid. It is easy to grow, with rich bright orange flowers flushed with black spots, opening in early summer.

- SITE The tiger lily prefers moist acid soil but will tolerate some lime. 'Enchantment' is easy to grow in a wide range of soil. Grow in borders or in containers where the flowers are in sunshine but the base has some shade. It will come up year after year.
- PROPAGATION The tiger lily is a clump-forming bulb which will multiply of its own accord.
- CULINARY USES Whole lily flowers give an aromatic flavour to poultry, especially duck. The petals can be torn and used either cooked to stuff fish or uncooked in a vinaigrette to dress a salad.
- FLOWER DISSECTION Eat the flower whole in cooked dishes or separated into petals. Use the petals only in salads.

Lilium lancifolium (tiger lily)

Melissa officinalis 'Aurea'
LEMON BALM

Lemon balm is a perennial plant found in southern Europe. It grows about 1m/3ft high and 45cm/18in across. In summer, leafy whorled spikes bear tiny, pale yellow to white, tubular flowers. The leaves are normally a dull green but there is also a golden variety called 'All Gold' as well as the golden variegated type. The flowers are so attractive to bees, that the plant is also known as bee balm (not to be confused with bergamot or red bee balm opposite).

- SITE Sunny, although light shade is appreciated for part of the day by variegated types. Can be grown in pots or in the garden. Fully hardy.
- PROPAGATION Sow seeds in a cold frame in the spring or divide plants in early spring or autumn.
- CULINARY USES The flowers are small but may be used in floral oils and salad dressings, or add them to chicken soup or stuffings. The leaves are extremely lemony in flavour and at their best when the flowers first open. Use them in all sorts of salads and vinaigrettes. An infusion can be made from the leaves, which is thought to alleviate cold symptoms and depression. Lemon balm is traditionally thought to contain the "elixir of life".
- FLOWER DISSECTION Eat the tiny, tubular flowers whole.

Mentha suaveolens
APPLE MINT

This is a widely distributed perennial, native to western and southern Europe growing up to 1m/3ft in height with an unrestricted spread. It flowers in summer in dense whorls bearing tiny pink or white tubular flowers. Pineapple mint is a very decorative variegated kind, with broad cream margins and a rich, pineapple fragrance. Many other varieties exist, including ginger mint, peppermint, spearmint and eau de cologne mint. All the flowers can be used to great effect and are a favourite with bees.

- SITE Sunny and moist. If planted in a herb bed, mint will need restricting or else it will take over. Excellent in containers, especially hanging baskets.
- PROPAGATION Sow seeds in spring. Small sections of mint root easily in water; pot up soon after roots appear. Divide roots in spring or autumn. Portions of rhizome will root anytime during the growing season – just pot up until established.
- CULINARY USES This flower combines easily with oils, vinegar and butter in sweet and savoury dishes. It is a winning combination with chocolate.
- FLOWER DISSECTION Individual florets should be removed from the stem, leaving the green parts behind. For making oil or vinegar or for decorative purposes use whole flower-heads.

Mentha spicata (spearmint)

Monarda didyma
BERGAMOT

Bergamot is a perennial plant from the prairies and woodlands of North America, where it is sometimes known as red bee balm. There are many garden cultivars including the pale pink 'Beauty of Cobham', the rose-pink 'Croftway Pink' and the red 'Cambridge Scarlet'. Wild bergamot, *Monarda fistulosa* has pale lavender-pink flowers and an intense flavour. They all generally grow about 1m/3ft high and 45cm/18in wide. Flowers in mid to late summer. Bees love them.

- SITE Full sun or light shade.
- PROPAGATION Sow seeds in spring. Divide clumps every two years in spring, prior to new growth.
- CULINARY USES As well as being colourful, the petals have a sweet, spicy flavour which means that, used sparingly, they will enhance all sorts of pasta and rice dishes. The flowers and leaves can be used in stuffings, salads and jellies. The Oswego Indians of North America infused bergamot to drink and the idea was copied by European settlers who used it as a tea substitute after the Boston Tea Party incident in 1773. Add 15ml/ 1 tbsp of young bergamot leaves to Earl Grey tea and enjoy the added flavour.
- FLOWER DISSECTION Each flower-head is made up of numerous tubular petals which can be pulled away individually and eaten whole. Pick newly opened flowers for the best results.

plant directory

Myrrhis odorata
SWEET CICELY

This is a stout perennial which grows fast in late spring, producing bright green pinnate leaves, often with a distinctive white blotch. The leaves, stems, and flowers all smell of aniseed when crushed which immediately distinguishes it from cow parsley which is resembles. It comes from southern Europe and can reach 2m/6ft and up to 1m/3ft across.

- SITE Moist, dappled shade.
- PROPAGATION Sow seeds in spring. Sow either in individual pots from which the young seedlings can be transplanted when all threat of frost has passed, or sow directly into garden soil or pots where they are to flower. This plant self-seeds with ease and although welcome in small numbers its deep roots make it difficult to remove. Best to remove semi-ripe seeds before they turn black.
- CULINARY USES The flowers taste deliciously of mild aniseed and can be used to add flavour to fish, green salads or fruit salads. Cook with roasted red (bell) peppers with the semi-ripe seeds. The leaves are often added to stewed rhubarb where they offset the tartness.
- FLOWER DISSECTION Sweet cicely is edible in many parts including flower, leaf, and semi-ripe seeds. The flower emerges in late spring and early summer and is best harvested very fresh. Just cut the flowers off the stem and use.

Myrrhis odorata (sweet cicely)

Ocimum basilicum
BASIL

Basil is an annual (or short-lived perennial) plant originally native to hot dry regions of subtropical Africa and Asia. It is now cultivated all over the world. It will grow 30–60cm/1–2ft high and 30–60cm/1–2ft across. In late summer, each flowering stem produces whorls of six small, tubular flowers. These are usually white although they may have a pink or purplish tinge. There are several purple-leaved varieties available including 'Purple Ruffles' and 'Dark opal'. These have attractive pink flowers. Basil complements tomatoes in the garden – it is the perfect companion plant and repels insects such as whitefly.

- SITE Full sun. Can be grown in pots or the garden. Only move outside from mid-summer onwards.
- PROPAGATION Sow seeds at 13ºC/55ºF in spring or directly in the garden in early summer.
- CULINARY USES The flowers are deliciously sweet and packed with clove-like flavour. Use them in floral oils, salad dressings, to add to soup and as a topping to roast aubergines (eggplants) and tomatoes. The leaves are wonderfully aromatic and an essential ingredient in pasta and pizza recipes.
- FLOWER DISSECTION Eat the tiny tubular flowers whole. They are beautifully sweet and very tasty. They come away easily from the green surrounds.

Oenothera biennis
EVENING PRIMROSE

Usually grown as a biennial, this plant originates from eastern North America but is now naturalized in many parts of the world. It grows 1–1.5m/3–5ft tall by 60cm/24in across. Cup-shaped, delicately fragrant flowers are produced from mid-summer to autumn, making it a welcome addition to the garden. Each flower, 5cm/2in across, opens in the evenings. They often stay out longer and longer as the season progresses.

- SITE Prefers sunny, dry conditions, although will adapt to many situations.
- PROPAGATION Easy to grow inside from seed sown in spring and planted out after all threat of frost has passed. In light soil it will self-seed with ease.
- CULINARY USES The gorgeous yellow flower tastes like lettuce, so makes a fine addition to any salad. The buds can be used as well for the same purpose. The leaf and stem were once popular with Native Americans for medicinal purposes. The seeds are used medicinally to relieve pre-menstrual discomfort. The root may be boiled and tastes like sweet parsnip, while the seeds can be used in baking, like poppy seeds.
- FLOWER DISSECTION The entire flower is edible, however, the evening primrose opens during the evening and generally closes after midday, so open flowers can be elusive. Buds can be eaten too.

Oenothera biennis (evening primrose)

Origanum vulgare
WILD MARJORAM/OREGANO

This is an aromatic woody-based perennial from Europe, growing on chalk and limestone outcrops. It reaches heights and spreads between 30–90cm/12–36in. It bears dense clusters of mauve, pink or white tubular flowers, only 4mm/⅛in long, from mid-summer to early autumn. Bees and butterflies, particularly the orange-tipped butterfly, are very attracted to it.

- SITE Full sun, except for golden marjoram which prefers partial shade, in well-drained, preferably alkaline, soil. Excellent for edging paths, in the herb garden or in containers.
- PROPAGATION Sow seeds in a cold frame in autumn or with a little heat in spring. Divide in spring or early autumn. It self-seeds with ease. It also roots from spreading prostrate branches which touch the soil.
- CULINARY USES This little aromatic flower combines well with all chicken dishes, as well as many fish recipes. Preserve the flowers in oil, vinegar or butter. Flowering tops make a good hot tea. The flowers complement traditional pizza ingredients. Scatter 15ml/1 tbsp of flowers over a pizza, drizzle marjoram oil over the edges and bake.
- FLOWER DISSECTION Pick the small, newly opened flowers either with or without the green parts behind. The flowers may be small but they are tasty.

Pelargonium
SCENTED GERANIUMS

Scented geraniums are tender evergreen perennials which, if kept in frost-free conditions, will mature into quite large bushes 0.3–1m /1–3ft high. They bear single mauve, pink, purple or white flowers during the summer months and well into the autumn if temperatures stay warm. The leaves are highly scented when touched; the flowers less so. The leaves may exude an orange scent as in 'Prince of Orange', lemon as in *P. crispum* 'Variegatum', or rose as in 'Attar of Roses' and P. 'Capitatum'. Other spicy fragrances include nutmeg.

- SITE Full sun. Excellent for pots and all types of containers which can be kept over the winter in frost-free conditions.
- PROPAGATION Take cuttings in spring or autumn from non-flowering shoots and put into small pots where they can establish roots.
- CULINARY USES The leaves have a powerful flavour and add a wonderful flavour to cakes and meringue roulades. The flowers are not especially flavoursome; picked when newly opened they have a faint flavour similar to the leaves, tasting slightly of citrus. Crystallize and scatter on top of desserts as a garnish.
- FLOWER DISSECTION Harvest the flowers when they first open. Remove the petals leaving all green parts behind.

Pelargonium (scented geranium)

Primula veris
COWSLIP

Cowslips are evergreen or semi-evergreen perennials which are found growing wild in the chalk, limestone or clay grasslands of Europe and western Asia. They are endangered but can be cultivated. Yellow flowers, like drooping primroses, appear in spring and grow in umbels at the top of long stems. Once pollinated the flowers turn upwards. They grow about 25cm/10in high and 25cm/10in across.

- SITE Sun or partial shade in moist, well-drained soil. Suitable for cottage borders, grassland or containers.
- PROPAGATION Sow seeds in a cold frame in early spring. Divide plants in late winter. They will self-seed in grass, gravel or borders.
- CULINARY USES Their beautiful honey smell makes them one of the most popular edible flowers. They may be pickled with sugar and white wine vinegar, or made into cowslip wine, often flavoured with orange and lemon. They can be added to a syrup of honey and water flavoured with lemon and sweet briar to make cowslip mead. The young leaves may be eaten in salads. They can be crystallized and used to decorate cowslip cream, cakes and cookies.
- FLOWER DISSECTION Gently pull the petals away from the long green calyxes. These are known as "pips", and should come away intact. Remove any green knobs at the lower end.

plant directory

plant directory

Primula vulgaris
PRIMROSE

The primrose is native to Europe and western Turkey. It is an evergreen or, in very dry seasons, a semi-evergreen perennial, which will self-seed freely and naturalize in partial shade. The pale yellow flowers appear in abundance from early to late spring. Established plants will grow about 35cm/14in across.

- SITE Partial shade. Grow in containers or in the garden, hedgerow or woodland.
- PROPAGATION It will self-seed in grass, woodland, gravel or borders. Can be divided in spring or autumn.
- CULINARY USES Use fresh on green salads or fruity meringues. Crystallize with egg white and sugar, and use to decorate cakes, cookies, roulades and trifles. Old recipes describe how to make a sweet primrose candy. Leaves may be used, either fresh or dried, to make tea. Use the flowers to make floral ice cubes or mix them with other spring flowers such as sweet violets, violas and cowslips to make a beautiful spring ice bowl. Serve a lemon sorbet inside it, decorated with whole crystallized primroses.
- FLOWER DISSECTION Gently remove petals from the stalk and surrounding green parts. They should all come away intact.

Primula vulgaris (primrose)

Rosa
ROSE

The wide variety of roses makes them perennially popular in the garden. Some will ramble, others climb, while others grow into bushy shrubs. Colours are myriad, including white, yellow, pink, red and orange. If the fragrance is powerful they are certainly worth eating. Pink 'Louise Odier' and 'Gertrude Jekyll' are two favourites, while the buttonhole rose, 'Cecile Brunner', with its tightly furled buds, looks sensational crystallized.

- SITE Sunny and moist. They are easy to grow in borders or in containers. 'Gertrude Jekyll' is wonderful in a wooden tub while many of the 'County Series' roses are perfect for planting in hanging baskets.
- PROPAGATION Take hardwood cuttings in early autumn and plant out in borders the following spring.
- CULINARY USES All rose flowers are edible and yet they vary enormously in flavour. Generally speaking those with the best scents will be the tastiest. To fully appreciate the flavour of your rose petals, crystallize them first. Make a batch of rose-petal jam, rose drop candies, damask rose syrup or honey of roses. Try musk roses with sugar and water to make rose water.
- FLOWER DISSECTION Pick the flower soon after opening. Gently pull the petals away from the centre of the flower and remove the white heel at the base.

Rosmarinus officinalis
ROSEMARY

This shrubby evergreen perennial originates from the sunny scrubland areas of the Mediterranean. The narrow leaves are powerfully aromatic. The flowers are produced on the upper leaf axils in late spring and early summer and grow abundantly over many weeks. Rosemary sometimes flowers again in the autumn. The flowers are only 1cm/½in long, but a very pretty blue with a good flavour. The colour varies quite considerably from 'Benenden Blue', with its brilliant blue flowers, to the pink-flowered 'Roseus' and 'Majorca Pink'.

- SITE Full sun.
- PROPAGATION Sow seed in a cold frame in spring. Root semi-ripe cuttings of non-flowering shoots in summer.
- CULINARY USES Rosemary flowers are both attractive and full of flavour so they have many different uses. Emphasize the sweetness by crystallizing them. Make rosemary butter for use on bagels and cheese crackers. Mix with creamed potato to eat with roast lamb or use as a topping on shepherd's pie. Transform a tomato salad with a drizzle of rosemary oil and a scattering of flowers. In the past, the leaves were used in a tonic.
- FLOWER DISSECTION Pick newly opened flowers and remove any green parts. The flowers taste like the leaf but also have a very sweet nectary taste at the base.

Rosmarinus officinalis (rosemary)

Salvia officinalis
SAGE

Sage comes from an enormous family of plants which is distributed widely throughout the world in both hot and temperate regions. Common sage is an evergreen perennial from the Mediterranean and North Africa which grows 80cm/32in tall and 1m/3ft wide. It has either grey, purple or variegated leaves with blue flowers.

- SITE Full sun or light shade in well-drained soil. Ideal for herb borders and containers.
- PROPAGATION Root from cuttings taken in late summer. Can also be grown outside from seed in early summer, after all threat of frost has gone.
- CULINARY USES The flowers taste like the leaves and are a valuable ingredient in the kitchen. They are ideal for oils, vinegar and butters and make a vibrant contribution to salads and pâtés as well as mustards and vinaigrettes. In the past, sage conserve was made using flowers with an equal weight of sugar. All sage flowers are edible, including clary sage (*Salvia sclarea*) and pineapple sage (*Salvia elegans*), so sweet they are a real delicacy. The flowers lose their colour and turn brown when cooked, so are best eaten raw.
- FLOWER DISSECTION The tubular flowers are easily pulled away from the long flowering stem. Remove any green or brown parts around the base.

Sambucus nigra
COMMON ELDER

This is an extremely hardy upright bushy shrub from Europe, north Africa and south-west Asia which grows to 6m/20ft tall and across. The heady musk-scented white flowers are borne in large numbers in early summer and are followed by huge trusses of black berries in autumn. There are golden, variegated and bronze-leaved forms. Their flowers and berries can be used in the same way as the common elder.

- SITE A sunny position, although will tolerate partial shade. Cut back growth if shrub grows too big.
- PROPAGATION Either by semi-ripe hardwood cuttings in summer from the new growth or by seed in the autumn.
- CULINARY USES Both elderflowers and berries are used to make wine, while the non-alcoholic elderflower cordial has been a great favourite for centuries. Tied in a muslin (cheesecloth) bag, and removed before serving, the flowers add a distinctive flavour to tarts, jellies and jams.
- FLOWER DISSECTION Pick newly opened flower-heads and immerse in salted water to clean off insects. Remove the stalks.

> **WARNING**
> Contact with the leaves may irritate the skin. Do not eat unripe berries. Ripe berries must always be cooked.

Sambucus nigra (common elder)

Taraxacum officinale
DANDELION

This is a perennial plant from the grasslands of northern and central Europe. It grows 20cm/8in high and 20cm/8in across. The flowers appear in early spring and continue through the summer.

- SITE Grassland, newly disturbed areas, pathways, borders; in fact almost anywhere!
- PROPAGATION This plant will be sure to appear without invitation and will happily self-seed.
- CULINARY USES The leaves can be blanched like chicory (Belgian endive), then shredded or chopped and used as a main salad ingredient. Use before the plant reaches flowering stage, thereafter the leaves are bitter. In the past, the whole plant, including the root, was used to make dandelion beer. The roots can be roasted and ground to make a dandelion coffee, while dandelion tea is made simply by pouring boiling water on the flowers. The flowers also make a good wine and the petals may be added to salads as decoration.
- FLOWER DISSECTION Leave the flower-head whole for use in wine, tea or salads but be sure to remove all green parts. The flowers close up quite quickly after picking so if intending to use them whole in salads, it is best to leave them until the last minute. Alternatively remove petals and use them individually.

plant directory

Thymus vulgaris
THYME

This is a hardy evergreen perennial plant from chalk and limestone grasslands of the western Mediterranean to southern Italy. It grows 15–30cm/6–12in high by 40cm/16in across and produces dense clusters of purple to white flowers. The leaves have a powerful scent especially when crushed. Try 'Doone Valley' with its lemon-scented gold-splashed leaves, or 'Citriodorus', also lemon scented.

- SITE Full sun. Thyme is a useful paving plant and is excellent in containers. Grow it with lavender in a summer herb hanging basket or with parsley and bay to make a bouquet garni.
- PROPAGATION Sow seeds in spring. Separate rooted stem sections in spring or summer.
- CULINARY USES Thyme is a very useful herb in the kitchen, and with parsley and bay, is an ingredient in a classic bouquet garni. The flowers have a strong flavour similar to the leaves which makes them ideal for producing thyme-flower oils, vinegars or butters, to use with freshly cooked vegetables such as carrots and mushrooms.
- FLOWER DISSECTION The flowers are very small and grow in dense clusters. Where individual flowers are needed, pull them carefully from the stem, leaving all green parts behind. The flower cluster may also be used whole.

Thymus vulgaris (thyme)

Tilia x europaea
LIME TREE

A large deciduous tree, native to a wide area of Europe, which can grow up to 35m/115ft high and 15m/50ft across. Other species include the American linden, *Tilia americana*, native to eastern North America. The different species interbreed naturally, resulting in hybrids. Drooping clusters of pale yellow flowers are borne in mid-summer. They have a celebrated fragrance and act as a mecca to bees, resulting in a honey with a distinctive flavour.

- SITE This is such a large tree that only very large gardens can grow it unless it is pleached regularly.
- PROPAGATION Sow seed as soon as it is ripe, into a seed bed, in autumn.
- CULINARY USES The most common use is lime-flower tea which is made from flowers, dried in the shade and then kept in a dry place in an airtight container. For every cup, add 5ml/1 tsp of flowers then allow it to infuse for just a few minutes. Strain and sweeten, if preferred, with honey. In the past, an orange leaf was often added for extra flavour. It has a soothing effect and helps induce sleep. Lime-blossom wine flavoured with lemon was another favourite.
- FLOWER DISSECTION The flowers should be picked just as they begin to open. Detach the flower from the stem and remove the stalks. They can be dried and kept for future use.

Trifolium pratense
CLOVER

Known as bee bread, red clover is highly attractive to bumble bees as well as other insects, including butterflies, moths and long-tongued flies. Red clover has large, dense globular heads made up of 30 or more petals. There are many strains of both red and white clover. They can all be used, but the red variety is the favourite for drinks.

- SITE Open sunny site; ideal for grassland.
- PROPAGATION Sow seed *in situ* in spring.
- CULINARY USES Scatter the petals on green or fruit salads, or use to make floral ice cubes. Whole flowers can be used to make clover wine, by combining equal quantities of clover flowers and boiling water, flavouring with orange and lemon rind and mixing with yeast. Red clover was used as a food by Native Americans. In parts of rural northern Europe, white clover petals and seeds were dried and ground in place of grains to make bread.
- FLOWER DISSECTION Use whole heads to make wine or a sleep-inducing tea. Pull the individual petals out of the flower-head to suck the sweetness from the base.

Trifolium pratense (clover)

Tropaeolum majus
NASTURTIUM

Nasturtiums are also commonly known as Indian cress and originate in Bolivia and Colombia. They are climbing annuals which may grow 1–3m/3–10ft tall. Many of the hybrids which are available today are much shorter. *T.* 'Jewel Series' grows only 30cm/12in high and has double and semi-double flowers; *T.* 'Gleam Series' is semi-trailing and grows up to 40cm/16in long. 'Empress of India' is another dwarf and has rich velvety red flowers. The flowers are generally about 8–10cm/3–4in across.

- SITE Full sun. Will flower profusely on impoverished soil or in a restricted container such as a hanging basket.
- PROPAGATION Sow seed in spring where it is to flower.
- CULINARY USES These vibrant flowers have a very strong peppery taste which makes them ideal for all sorts of garnishes, salads and pasta dishes. Those that have long spurs at the base of the flowers are amazingly sweet at the end of the tips, giving a wonderfully peppery-sweet combination. The leaves and flowers of all annual nasturtiums can be eaten and the young fruits pickled as a caper substitute.
- FLOWER DISSECTION The flowers can be eaten whole or, for a milder taste, separate the petals from the base and just eat the petals. Pick newly opened flowers for best results.

Viola odorata
SWEET VIOLET

Either blue or white, this sweetly scented violet is a semi-evergreen perennial from southern and western Europe which will self-seed freely and naturalize in partial shade. The flowers appear in late winter to early spring, growing about 8–10cm/3–4in high, then the leaves grow bigger and eventually cover the flowers. Plants will eventually form clumps about 30cm/12in across. 'Parma' violets are very highly scented forms, which have an exquisite fragrance and flavour. They may be blue, pink, violet or white and are available in both single and double forms.

- SITE Partial shade. Grow in containers or in the garden, hedgerow or woodland.
- PROPAGATION It will self-seed. Can be divided in spring or autumn.
- CULINARY USES The gentle flavour partners well with savoury and sweet foods. Use fresh on salads or pâtés or crystallize with egg white and sugar, and use to decorate cakes, cookies, roulades and desserts. Infuse with vinegar to make a vinaigrette to use as a dressing on salads or seafood. In the past violets were cooked to make a sweet paste or candy. Leaves may be used either fresh or dried to make tea.
- FLOWER DISSECTION The flowers each have five petals, about 2cm/¾in across. Gently remove petals from stalk and surrounding green parts.

Viola odorata (sweet violet)

Viola
VIOLA

Violas are related to sweet violets but have a larger flower and later flowering period, blooming from spring through to mid-summer in a range of colours ranging from white, cream, yellow, purple, blue and several bicolours. Many of them are sweetly scented. Several varieties are recommended, including black 'Mollie Sanderson', blue-edged 'Rebecca' and white 'Mrs Lancaster'. However, there are numerous others – in order to reach a decision, choose scented varieties. Remove flowers as they fade in order to prolong the flowering period. They are perfect for hanging baskets, flowering on and off throughout the summer.

- SITE Sun or partial shade or full shade.
- PROPAGATION Sow seeds in a cold frame in early autumn or take cuttings of non-flowering shoots in July.
- CULINARY USES The flowers do not have a strong flavour but they have such a pretty appearance, often with strong bee-like markings, that they make a good contribution to any salad or as a garnish on a pâté. They can be crystallized and used on cakes, cookies or creamy desserts. Use to make floral ice cubes or a pretty summer ice bowl filled with sorbets or ice creams.
- FLOWER DISSECTION Remove flowers from stems and discard green parts.

plant directory

index

AUTHOR'S ACKNOWLEDGEMENTS

I would like to give very special thanks to Michelle Garrett for her endless patience in taking these stunning photographs, also to Joanna Farrow for her inspiring and glorious interpretation of the food recipes. I would particularly like to show my gratitude to Lindsay Porter, my editor, who gave such wonderful support throughout the making of this book. Also, of course, heartfelt thanks to Simon, Jonathan and Suzanna for their endless ways of helping with this project, including the tasting of so many glorious flowers.

PICTURE CREDITS

A–Z Botanical page 146 bottom left; Bridgeman Art Library page 10; Edimedia page 15; Fine Art Photographic Library pages 11, 14 top right; Garden Picture Library page 150 bottom right; Mary Evans Picture Library pages 12, 14 bottom left, 16, 17.